Insider intel from
dog lover to dog lover—

DOG-FRIENDLY

LONDON

Compiled by—
MARTA ROCA

Photography by—
LESLEY LAU
DUNJA OPALKO
ARIANA RUTH

Written by—
KAREN DAY
OLIVIA FINLAYSON
HANNAH SUMMERS

Profiles by—
CHLOË ASHBY

Illustrations by—
PAULINE CREMER

FOUR&SONS✕**HOXTON MINI PRESS**

This guide features a selection
of our favourite dog-friendly places
in London. It's not a comprehensive
listing as much as a collection of insider
intel (from dog lover to dog lover) to help
you discover the boroughs (and beyond)
with your four-legged friends.

Although we aim to be as accurate as
possible with the information provided,
please always refer to up-to-date
details, rules, or regulations, including
restricted areas and hotel or restaurant
policies, when planning to visit with
your four-legged friends.

WELCOME TO LONDON

London is the kind of place where people are more likely to say hello to a pup than a person. Perhaps that's an exaggeration, but it's definitely true that Londoners love dogs. Here, you'll find snub-nosed French bulldogs in artsy bookshops, whippets happily snoozing under a table at your local pub, Labradors joyously bounding in Hampstead Heath, beagles being spoilt with room service, and Dalmatians dressed in the finest cashmere sweaters. If you're ready to discover what this city has to offer when your pup's leading the way, we've got you covered. All breeds welcome.

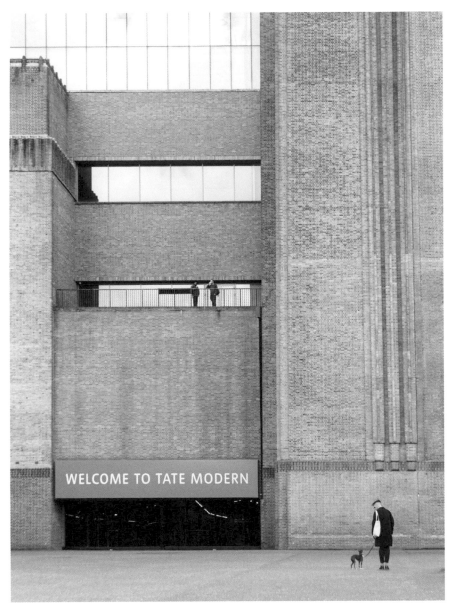

WELCOME TO TATE MODERN

WALK

A walk around London can range from a casual pavement stroll in boho neighbourhoods to a run with the pack in one of the city's 3,000—yes, that's 3,000—parks. The surplus of green spaces offers something for every sort of wayfarer with a wagging tail: secluded squares, wild heaths, historic cemeteries, canal-side gardens, and sprawling royal grounds where kings and queens once rode horses. Whether your hound loves to sniff, play, or squirrel-chase, there's always somewhere exciting to take them. Or, better yet, see where they lead you.

Regent's Canal

GREENWICH PARK
GREENWICH

Even Queen Elizabeth I was taken by the beauty of Greenwich Park— she used to picnic beneath the shade of an ancient oak tree now named in her honour, that although fallen, still can be viewed. Today the park is popular for its tree-lined paths, pretty boating lake, and a great little café, perfect for an afternoon tea if the weather's being typically British. On a nice day, spend time taking in the views or exploring the stunning rose garden at Ranger's House, a Georgian Palladian mansion.

GRAB A COFFEE AT

GREENWICH GRIND
17–19 NELSON ROAD
SE10 9JB
—

DOGS ARE NOT PERMITTED AT
FLOWER AND ROSE GARDENS
THE WILDERNESS DEER PARK
THE ROYAL OBSERVATORY GARDEN

ON-LEAD ONLY AREAS
RANGER'S HOUSE GARDEN

LONDON SE10 8QY
ROYALPARKS.ORG.UK
@THEROYALPARKS

EAST AND WEST
Another (touristy but fun) highlight sits on the grounds of the Royal Observatory, where you can pose with your pooch on the prime meridian line. You can put two paws and one foot in both the eastern and western hemispheres.

ABNEY PARK CEMETERY
STOKE NEWINGTON

This ever-so-slightly eerie north London cemetery, built in the early 1800s and known as one of the 'Magnificent Seven' cemetries of the capital to architectural historians, makes for a unique walk with your pup. It was initially laid out as an exotic arboretum, with over 2,500 varieties of plants and trees planted alphabetically by species, many of them original, around the perimeter. Today, it offers lots of interesting smells for dogs and some of the best bird-spotting in the city. It's the tranquil resting place of many Londoners, and the Gothic chapel in the centre is the oldest surviving non-denominational chapel in Europe.

GRAB A COFFEE AT

YELLOW WARBLER COFFEE
9 NORTHWOLD ROAD
N16 7HL
—

215 STOKE NEWINGTON HIGH STREET
N16 0LH
ABNEYPARK.ORG
@ABNEYPARKN16

HYDE PARK AND KENSINGTON GARDENS
KENSINGTON

From Henry VIII to Lady Diana, Hyde Park has had its fair share of royal fans. And rightly so. This 350-acre green space (one of three city parks that make up the 'Lungs of London') is criss-crossed with paths linking fountains, statues, gardens, and wide, tree-lined boulevards. At Rotten Row, the sandy bridleway running the length of Hyde Park's south side, you and your dog can catch cavalry horses prancing about during their morning exercise. During summer, leave all the regal fanfare behind to see what's on at the Serpentine Pavilion, an architectural showcase in the park. On your way out, pass by dog-loving Virginia Woolf's childhood home. It's handily located on a side street close to the Royal Albert Hall gate entrance—just look for the famous blue plaque.

GRAB A COFFEE AT

THE GENTLEMEN BARISTAS
34 BRUTON PLACE
W1J 6NR
—

DOGS ARE NOT PERMITTED AT
DIANA MEMORIAL FOUNTAIN
LIDO SWIMMING AREA
THE SERPENTINE LAKE
BOWLING GREEN AND TENNIS AREA
LONG WATER
ROUND POND
PETER PAN STATUE

ON-LEAD ONLY AREAS
ROSE GARDEN
EDGE OF THE SERPENTINE LAKE
EDGE OF ROUND POND AND LONG WATER
AROUND THE ITALIAN GARDENS
SOUTH FLOWER WALK
NORTH FLOWER WALK

ROYALPARKS.ORG.UK
@THEROYALPARKS

LINCOLN'S INN FIELDS
HOLBORN

London's biggest public square provides peaceful respite in the middle of the city. Named after the adjoining Lincoln's Inn, an impressive set of historic red-brick buildings and one of four Inns of Court for the city's judges and barristers, it's not your classic dog-walking spot—but that's why we love it. Great Turnstile and Little Turnstile are the alleyways that connect the field to High Holborn, and were used as actual turnstiles to prevent cattle straying from the area up until the 17th century. In this century it's all about on-lead saunters around the park's perimeter, chasing a pigeon or two as you go. If you find yourself here sans pup, pay a visit to the house and museum of British architect Sir John Soane across the street.

GRAB A COFFEE AT

PRUFROCK COFFEE
23-25 LEATHER LANE
EC1N 7TE

—

WC2A 3ED
PARKSANDGARDENS.ORG

DULWICH PARK
DULWICH

A quaint village vibe has made the semi-rural streets around Dulwich Park some of the most sought-after in the city—no wonder that some of Britain's best writers, actors, and comedians call these leafy streets home. It's tempting to pound the pavement, ogling the area's multi-million-pound townhouses, but the park is the place where dogs can roam happily, and safely, off lead, diving into the lake, sniffing around the gardens, or charging across the grass. Go rub fur with other polished pooches in the park's café before stopping in across the road at Dulwich Picture Gallery, which welcomes well-behaved pups to its grounds.

GRAB A COFFEE AT

GAIL'S
91 DULWICH VILLAGE
SE21 7BJ

—

COLLEGE ROAD
SE21
SOUTHWARK.GOV.UK
DULWICHPARKFRIENDS.ORG.UK
@DULWICHPARK_FRIENDS

VICTORIA PARK
HACKNEY

Vicky Park, as it's lovingly called by locals, is arguably London's hippest green hangout. Designed 'for the people' in 1841, the park and its 4,500 trees have witnessed everything from political speeches and music gigs to prosecco-fuelled picnics and trendy running clubs that make a 5K somehow seem fun. Many of the park's historical features were destroyed in World War II, but beauty remains, including an impressive Victorian-era drinking fountain and a large boating lake. If you come in through the canal-side entrance at Bonner Gate, you and your pup can greet dogs of another kind: statues of the park's guards, the Dogs of Alcibiades. A version of these two marble wardens has stood here since 1912 (the originals are now in the British Museum).

GRAB A COFFEE AT

PAVILION CAFÉ
VICTORIA PARK
OLD FORD ROAD
E9 7DE
—

GROVE ROAD
E3 5TB
PARKSANDGARDENS.ORG

PAVILION CAFÉ
Grab a pastry for you, and a couple of homemade oat, pumpkin, and banana treats for the hound, before heading out to explore. A much-loved pit stop on any east London dog walk.

HAMPSTEAD HEATH
HAMPSTEAD

Wild and wonderful, the Heath is
a vast stretch of heather, gardens, and
woodland covering close to 800 acres.
Pack a picnic and get lost among
the hauntingly beautiful old trees or
aimlessly wander and wonder at what
you, and your dog, discover. Back on the
trail, make your way to Parliament Hill.
It can get crowded up there, but
for good reason: you can gaze out at the
London skyline from what seems like
arm's length. Bask in the uninterrupted
city view, then head to Highgate No.1
Pond to let your hound cool off with
a leisurely splash-about.

GRAB A COFFEE AT

THE NOOK
43 SOUTH END ROAD
NW3 2PY
—

DOGS ARE NOT PERMITTED AT
HILL GARDEN AND PERGOLA

ON-LEAD ONLY AREAS
GOLDERS HILL PARK

CITYOFLONDON.GOV.UK
@COLHAMPSTEADHEATH
HAMPSTEADHEATH.NET

NO.1 POND
The Heath really does have it all:
ample green space, incredible
views, and a natural pond for dogs
to splash around.

ROUND IN CIRCLES

Pack some water and take your pup for a trek around the Heath. The four- to six-mile-long 'circular walk' is a slow-paced way to take in scenery while tiring out dogs who can go the distance.

BATTERSEA PARK
BATTERSEA

The Battersea area has a long history
of caring for the health and happiness
of animals. For starters, the world's first
successful animal rescue, Battersea
Dogs and Cats Home, has resided just
south-east of Battersea Park since 1871.
Today the tree-filled riverside space
is becoming increasingly upscale,
and it's now the stomping ground
of perfectly coiffed locals—we're talking
dogs as well as humans, of course.
Keep strolling south to extend your walk
around Clapham Common.

GRAB A COFFEE AT

DOPPIO
336 BATTERSEA PARK ROAD
SW11 3BY
—

LONDON SW11 4NJ
WANDSWORTH.GOV.UK
@BATTERSEAPARKLONDON

WILDLIFE
The park is home to a children's zoo, while adults may remember the inflatable pink pig once hovering over Battersea Power Station on the cover of Pink Floyd's *Animals*.

PECKHAM RYE PARK
AND COMMON
PECKHAM

Beyond the independent eateries
that have helped cement Peckham as
one of London's most vibrant hangouts
is Peckham Rye Park and Common,
where you're as likely to catch an
impromptu steel drum gig as you are
a sports match. The expanse of the
common is great for energetic dogs
who enjoy a serious bout of off-lead
zoomies, but as a picnic hotspot in
the summer, make sure you've got
good recall—tasty temptations abound.
If you're after a slower pace, head to
the park for a serene saunter through
the Japanese and American gardens
or simply chill out on a bench as you
watch skaters try to catch air on the
five-foot mini ramp.

GRAB A COFFEE AT

OLD SPIKE ROASTERY
54 PECKHAM RYE
SE15 4JR

—

DOGS ARE NOT PERMITTED AT
ARBORETUM

STRAKER'S ROAD
SE15 3UA
SOUTHWARK.GOV.UK
PECKHAMRYEPARK.ORG
@PECKHAMRYEPARK

RICHMOND PARK
RICHMOND

Richmond Park's sprawling 2,500-acre space was enclosed as a deer park by King Charles I in 1637, and there are still hundreds of the animals roaming here, along with every hound's favourite frenemies: squirrels and rabbits. The raw and rugged beauty makes this space one of the country's most memorable city parks. Shaded woodland, heaths, and duck-filled ponds give it a rural ramble vibe in its middle, while a brisk, 7.5-mile-long stroll around the perimeter can tire out even the hardiest of hounds. In need of more time out in nature? Bushy Park, in nearby Hampton, is a great add-on to make a longer day of it.

GRAB A COFFEE AT

GROUND COFFEE SOCIETY
79 LOWER RICHMOND ROAD
SW15 1ET

—

DOGS ARE NOT PERMITTED AT
PEMBROKE LODGE AND GARDENS

MAY TO JULY
DURING THE DEER BIRTHING SEASON
DOGS MUST BE KEPT ON LEADS
THROUGHOUT THE PARK

ROYALPARKS.ORG.UK
@THEROYALPARKS

DOGS AND DEER
Remember, your dog still has animal instincts. During birthing season, use a lead throughout this wonderful deer-filled park.

GUIDED WALK

SOUTH BANK
WATERLOO BRIDGE
TO TOWER BRIDGE

WITH LUIS REINA ROMAO,
ASHLEY BALL, AND YOKO

Take in London's motley architecture along the South Bank by walking
from Waterloo to Tower bridge, with a few key spots in between.
1 Gaze at the diagonals of the National Theatre and the layered
blocks holding up the Hayward Gallery, two of the city's best-loved
Brutalist buildings. **2** Let your pup paddle out at Thames Beach,
a shoreline that puts St. Paul's on the horizon with the sprawling lawns
of Bernie Spain Gardens behind it. **3** Stretch out and look up to see
OXO Tower. The Art Deco structure looks great by day and even better
at night, when it's lit up in neon. **4** Make your way past Tate Modern
to a reconstructed version of **5** one of the world's most celebrated
theatres, Shakespeare's Globe. Treat yourself—and your pup—
to cheese, charcuterie, and pastries at **6** Borough Market, the city's
oldest food market. Walk it off with a 15-minute stroll towards a
caffeine fix: **7** WatchHouse serves up 'modern coffee' in a minimalist,
dog-friendly shop. Back outside, you're steps from **8** Shad Thames,
an area home to the largest warehouse complex in London during
Victorian times. Today, many of the repurposed buildings hold original
features. On weekends, head from the river to Maltby Street Market,
where food stalls are lined up beneath 19th-century railway arches.

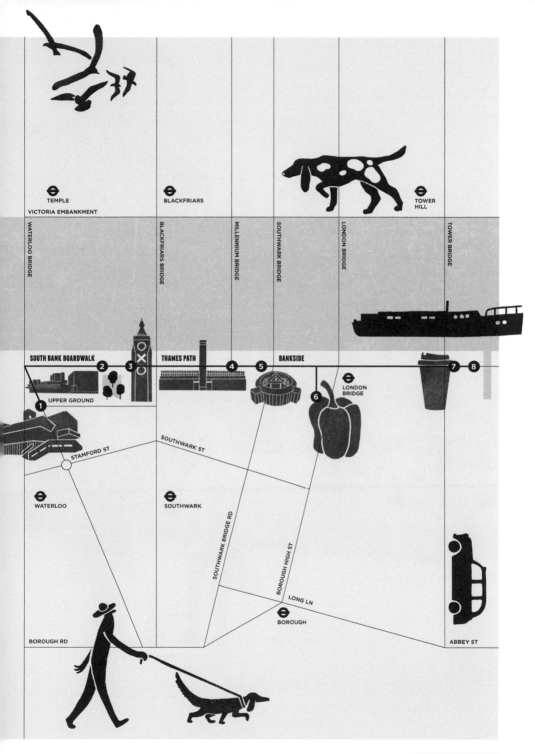

TEMPLE

VICTORIA EMBANKMENT

BLACKFRIARS

TOWER HILL

WATERLOO BRIDGE

BLACKFRIARS BRIDGE

MILLENNIUM BRIDGE

SOUTHWARK BRIDGE

LONDON BRIDGE

TOWER BRIDGE

SOUTH BANK BOARDWALK

THAMES PATH

BANKSIDE

UPPER GROUND

LONDON BRIDGE

STAMFORD ST

SOUTHWARK ST

WATERLOO

SOUTHWARK

SOUTHWARK BRIDGE RD

BOROUGH HIGH ST

LONG LN

BOROUGH

BOROUGH RD

ABBEY ST

TOP RIGHT
Tower Bridge

BELOW RIGHT
Shad Thames

OPPOSITE PAGE
Bankside overlooking
Tower Bridge

TOP LEFT
Hayward Gallery

BELOW LEFT
Thames Beach

OPPOSITE PAGE
Millennium Bridge
overlooking Tate Modern

EAST LONDON
COLUMBIA ROAD TO VICTORIA PARK

WITH MARTIN USBORNE,
BUG, AND MOOSE

Forget covering miles and miles: this compact walk takes in some of the finest shops, eateries, parks, and markets in arty East London. Consider these standouts a jumping-off point—the fun is in not knowing what else you may stumble across. **1** From vintage champagne coupes to colourful plant pots, start with a stroll around the indie shops of Columbia Road. If it's Sunday, you're here for the flower market, one of the best in the country. **2** Pop into Hackney Essentials and fill your tote with spicy 'nduja, jars of kimchi, and organic fruit and veg. **3** Just around the corner, let Campania & Jones transport you and the dog to southern Italy for a lunch of regional classics and daily handmade pasta. **4** Dessert is just across the street at Lily Vanilli Bakery. Colourful cake creations may be the speciality, but the gooey vegan brownies are not to be passed up. **5** Balance it out with a stroll through Haggerston Park. **6** A few minutes away, Ozone Coffee Roasters will satisfy any caffeine cravings and fix that mid-afternoon lull. Pick up a bag of beans for a perfect pour-over at home. **7** Add a detour to explore Broadway Market's myriad of merchants (don't miss beloved bookstore Artwords) before following **8** the canal down to **9** Victoria Park, where several off-lead areas mean you can tire out your pup with a game of fetch or a runaround with Hackney's four-legged hipsters. **10** At Pavilion Café, inside the park, a sneaky scrap of sausage roll with some pondside duck-spotting is a great end-of-day treat for your well-behaved hound.

LONDON FIELDS

7

BROADWAY MARKET

VICTORIA PARK RD

VICTORIA
PARK

10

9

PRITCHARD'S RD

8

BISHOPS WAY

6

CAMBRIDGE
HEATH

HAGGERSTON PARK

GOLDSMITH'S ROW

5

HACKNEY RD

OLD FORD RD

WARNER PL

HOXTON

CAMBRIDGE HEATH RD

3

4

2

COLUMBIA RD

GOSSET ST

SQUIRRIES ST

BETHNAL
GREEN

1

BETHNAL GREEN RD

WEAVERS FIELDS

BETHNAL
GREEN
GARDENS

BREATHING SPACE

From compact Haggerston Park to sprawling Hackney Marshes, east London offers pups plenty of green spaces to explore.

TOP LEFT
Pavilion Café

LEFT
Regent's Canal

OPPOSITE PAGE
Haggerston Park

PECKHAM

WITH NADJA OCCAM PENFOLD
AND SEYMOUR

Hop from independent shops to galleries, cafés, and bars on this laid-back tour of the best sights and dog-worthy smells in south-east London. **1** From flaky croissants to natural yoghurt, breakfast is covered at the General Store. Take a seat on the bench outside this grocery shop and then **2** hop over to Copeland Gallery, where an ever-changing roster of exhibitions and events take over this bright-white space. **3** Next door, at Peckham Supply, you can pick up shirts, beanies, ceramics, and other hard-to-resist knick-knacks. **4** It wouldn't be a Peckham tour without plenty of foodie stop-offs. Lunch is avocado and salsa matcha on toast at Nola, a dog-obsessed, Scandi-style café. **5** At Sage Flowers you'll find bespoke bunches and a riot of colour: step inside this lovely shop that turns its back on tradition and goes big on unusual flowers and foliage. If your pup's had enough pavement pounding, head to **6** Peckham Rye Park and Common for a runaround with the squirrels. For a treat of your own, circle back north to **7** Social bar at Copeland Park & Bussey Building. Grab a pew and guzzle a London-brewed craft beer or Hawkes cider. When you're ready to add food into the mix, head to **8** Coal Rooms, where dinner is cooked in a charcoal oven. Tuck your dog under your chair and stay for a while. You'll both feel warm and cosy here.

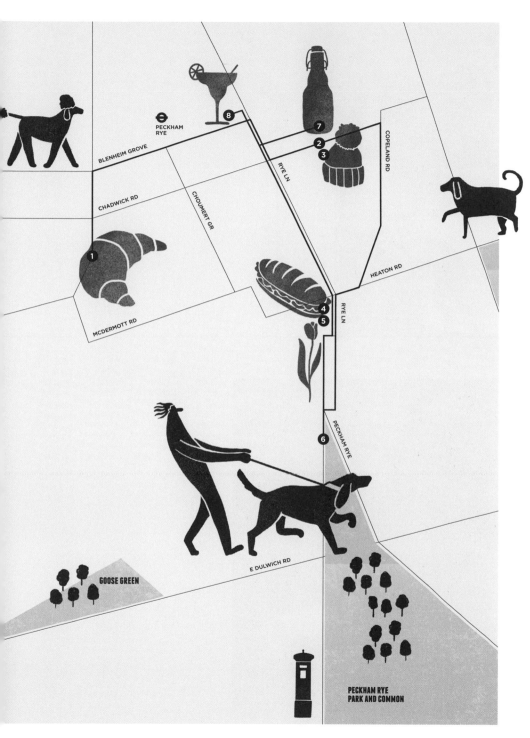

PECKHAM RYE

BLENHEIM GROVE

RYE LN

COPELAND RD

CHADWICK RD

CHOUMERT GR

HEATON RD

RYE LN

MCDERMOTT RD

PECKHAM RYE

E DULWICH RD

GOOSE GREEN

PECKHAM RYE
PARK AND COMMON

**COPELAND PARK &
BUSSEY BUILDING**

This progressive, mixed-use
space was built as a sporting
goods factory in 1887. Today it's
Peckham's community-driven
cultural hub.

TOP LEFT
Sage Flowers

BELOW LEFT
Peckham Rye Park

OPPOSITE PAGE
Copeland Park &
Bussey Building

TOP LEFT
Copeland Park &
Bussey Building

TOP RIGHT
Peckham Supply

BELOW RIGHT
Nola

OPPOSITE PAGE
Peckham Rye Park

REGENT'S CANAL
LITTLE VENICE
TO KING'S CROSS

WITH NIKO DAFKOS,
PAUL FIRMIN, AND PIPER

A leisurely stroll along the towpath of this famous north London canal—once used to transport cargo by horse—now reveals hidden gardens, brilliantly varied architecture, and some of the city's best coffee and cocktails. **1** Stroll through the greenhouses at Clifton Nurseries. The city's oldest garden centre has been inspiring green-fingered Londoners since 1851. **2** Cross over Blomfield Road to enter Little Venice, a colourful and eclectic mini neighbourhood along the canal. **3** Stop by Rembrandt Gardens, where in Spring you'll see thousands of multi-coloured tulips and hyacinths, before recharging at **4** D1 Coffee. Use the energy from their zingy espresso to skirt the edge of **5** Regent's Park, passing the ZSL London Zoo as you head towards the immaculate slopes of **6** Primrose Hill. Pause for a picture of your pup with the city skyline behind. Rejoin the canal and meander through Camden until you reach **7** the towering cast-iron frame at Gasholder Park. **8** As you reach Coal Drops Yard, pop into dog-friendly Earl of East to pick up candles, ceramics, and books before grabbing an al fresco lunch at Caravan, inside the Granary Building. The repurposed structure once stored Lincolnshire wheat for the city's bakers—today it's also home to the prestigious **9** Central Saint Martins art school. Do some people-watching at **10** Granary Square, where your dog can cool off in the fountains of this buzzy bar-lined space.

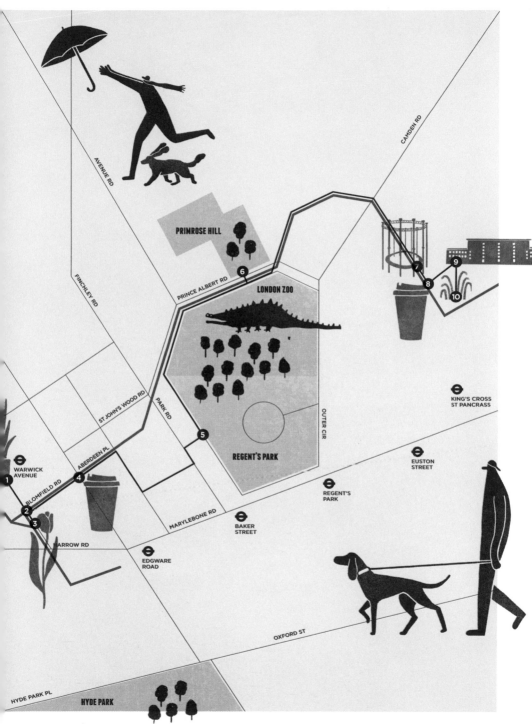

PRIMROSE HILL

PRINCE ALBERT RD

LONDON ZOO

CAMDEN RD

AVENUE RD

FINCHLEY RD

ST JOHN'S WOOD RD

PARK RD

ABERDEEN PL

BLOMFIELD RD

WARWICK
AVENUE

FARROW RD

EDGWARE
ROAD

MARYLEBONE RD

BAKER
STREET

REGENT'S PARK

OUTER CIR

REGENT'S
PARK

EUSTON
STREET

KING'S CROSS
ST PANCRASS

OXFORD ST

HYDE PARK PL

HYDE PARK

DOG-FRIENDLY LONDON **53**

TOP RIGHT
Elnathan Mews

BELOW RIGHT
Primrose Hill

OPPOSITE PAGE
Regent's Canal

ON THE TOWPATH

Regent's Canal opened in 1820 as a way to link King's Cross to commercial trade. It brought coal and goods to London from industrial cities in the Midland and North England. Today, it's a prime spot for a leafy stroll.

TOP RIGHT
Gasholder Park

TOP LEFT
Rembrandt Gardens

BELOW
Regent's Canal

OPPOSITE PAGE
Coal Drops Yard

STAY

Super-king beds with feather-filled pillows, a room service menu that begs you to stay in, and buzzing bars a few floors below. When it comes to a sleepover in this city, there are plenty of perks for you and your four-legged guest, too. Take your pick from hotels offering memory foam dog beds, the most polished of marble hallways for mucky paws to pad across, and a team ready to arrange anything for your dog— a coiffing of the fur or a sitter while you go out and explore. Whether you are planning a vacation or a staycation, this pup-loving capital is always best enjoyed with your four-legged friend at your heel.

THE HOXTON HOTEL
SOUTHWARK
ALSO IN HOLBORN
AND SHOREDITCH

Just south of the river and not far from
other go-to locations along the South
Bank such as Tate Modern and Borough
Market, the Hoxton Southwark blends
a relaxed and buzzy hotel vibe thanks
to the easy-going team and boozy
corners. The subtly retro rooms,
with velvet headboards and cosy wood
panelling, might inspire you and your
dog to opt for a night in, but the hotel's
knack for attracting locals—who come
to chatter over a low-key live DJ set—
will likely call you back downstairs.
During the day, the hotel's prime
riverside location makes it a spot for
freelancers who appreciate working
from mid-century armchairs and with
endless coffee on order. The Hoxton's
in-the-know team will fill you in on
the little back streets to explore or set
you up with a dog sitter so you're free
to linger over seafood and ceviche
in Seabird, the 14th-floor restaurant.

DOG-FRIENDLY DETAILS
NO ADDITIONAL FEE
DOG BED AND BOWLS PROVIDED
TREATS AVAILABLE ON REQUEST
LOCAL DOG-CENTRIC GUIDE
PET WAIVER REQUIRED
—
SOUTHWARK
40 BLACKFRIARS ROAD
SE1 8NY

HOLBORN
199–206 HIGH HOLBORN
WC1V 7BD

SHOREDITCH
81 GREAT EASTERN STREET
EC2A 3HU

THEHOXTON.COM
@THEHOXTONHOTEL

MUTT MANUAL
The Hox encourages canine–human
adventures with its local guide,
illustrated by British artist Alice
Bowsher. It's a brilliant jumping-off
point for getting to know the
neighbourhood's pup-friendly
establishments (as well as handy info
like vets, groomers, and dog walkers).

THE STANDARD, LONDON
KING'S CROSS

This Brutalist beauty on Euston Road once lived life as the Camden Town Hall Annexe. Today, the building is more about parties than paperwork, all with your pooch by your side. Designer Shawn Hausman (the creative behind NYC's outlandish nightclub Area) has underlined that sentiment by pulling together a festive atmosphere of brightly hued, retro interiors inspired by London tube seats. But don't worry if partying isn't your thing. You'll find books organised by subject, low-slung chairs, and plenty of calming plants in the library lounge. Or, you can upgrade your stay to a Junior Suite Terrace and relax in an outdoor bathtub. If it weren't for the view of King's Cross below, you might wonder if you're in London or LA.

DOG-FRIENDLY DETAILS
NO ADDITIONAL FEE
DOGS UNDER 10KG ALLOWED
TREATS AVAILABLE
PET WAIVER REQUIRED
DOGS MAY NOT BE LEFT UNATTENDED IN ROOMS
—

10 ARGYLE STREET
WC1H 8EG
STANDARDHOTELS.COM/LONDON
@THESTANDARDLONDON

ROSEWOOD LONDON
HOLBORN

With its ornate façade and grand entrance, you'd be forgiven for thinking you'd arrived at a swish country pad, not an Edwardian mansion transformed into an unapologetically luxurious hotel: inside, it's all neutral tones and plenty of marble. Bags are discreetly whisked away while your pup is given a loving stroke by softly spoken staff: four-legged guests are as important here as their humans. All guest rooms—decked out in plush carpets and fluffed pillows—are dog-friendly, along with the brasserie-style Holborn Dining Room, with its show-stopping pies, and Scarfes bar, where you can both settle in front of a roaring fire for an evening of killer cocktails.

DOG-FRIENDLY DETAILS
NO ADDITIONAL FEE
CANINE PACKAGE
—

252 HIGH HOLBORN
WC1V 7EN
ROSEWOODHOTELS.COM
@ROSEWOODLONDON

CANINE PACKAGE

For the ultimate indulgence, book the canine package, which includes Barbour amenities, dog sitting, and an hour with celebrated groomer Jamie Griffen.

THE PILGRM
PADDINGTON

Every dog owner knows holidays have a downside, and this is the reason: it's time away from your favourite fur buddy. Take your dog with you to the Pilgrm, a stunning set of digs in the heart of Paddington. Four Victorian townhouses have been transformed into 73 hip—yet affordable—hotel rooms, just one of the ways in which the Pilgrm is flipping hospitality on its head. Another is the lobby, or lack thereof; instead, guests enter through a ground floor café, and a fantastic one at that. The unexpected continues to the Terrace, where views of people pouring from Paddington Station are best complemented by cheese, cocktails, and blissful contentment for human and hound.

DOG-FRIENDLY DETAILS
FEE: £30 FOR STAY
DOGS UNDER 10KG ALLOWED
DOG BOWLS AVAILABLE ON REQUES
DOGS NOT ALLOWED IN CAFÉ OR LOUNGE
ONE DOG PER ROOM ONLY
—

25 LONDON STREET
W2 1HH
THEPILGRM.COM
@THEPILGRM

KINGSLAND LOCKE
DALSTON
ALSO IN ALDGATE,
MILLENNIUM BRIDGE,
AND TOWER BRIDGE

It's home-meets-hotel for humans and hounds at these pastel-hued apartments in Dalston. This is a space to experience the city in truly independent style—filling the fridge with your purchases from Broadway Market, cooking up a late breakfast, and lazing around on a green velvet sofa the morning after a big night out. This is Dalston, after all. Handily, it's filled with dog-friendly restaurants and dimly lit cocktail bars, making Locke ideally located for human-canine culinary exploration. If your stay is more business than pleasure, a plant-adorned co-working space, fully equipped gym, and on-site microbrewery will keep you in good company even when you can't wander about.

DOG-FRIENDLY DETAILS
**FEE: £25–£35 FOR STAY
DOGS UNDER 20KG ALLOWED
ONE DOG PER ROOM ONLY
PET WAIVER REQUIRED
BED, BOWLS, AND TREATS
AVAILABLE ON REQUEST**
—

KINGSLAND LOCKE
**130 KINGSLAND HIGH STREET
E8 2LQ**

BERMONDS LOCKE
**157 TOWER BRIDGE ROAD
SE1 3LW**

LEMAN LOCKE
**15 LEMAN STREET
E1 8EN**

LOCKE AT BROKEN WHARF
**BROKEN WHARF HOUSE
2 BROKEN WHARF
EC4V 3DT**

**LOCKELIVING.COM
@LOCKEHOTELS**

OTHER NOTEWORTHY HOTELS

ARTIST RESIDENCE
PIMLICO

Aficionados of the Aesthetic Movement, this one's for you. Located within a stone's throw of the Tate Britain, Artist Residence is a 10-room hotel where reclaimed wood, salvaged industrial treasures, mismatched furniture, and art (of course) abound. Dogs are welcome and will only serve to enhance the fabulously eclectic decor.

DOG-FRIENDLY DETAILS
FEE: £15 PER PET PER NIGHT
BED, BOWLS, AND TREATS INCLUDED
DOGS MAY NOT BE LEFT
UNATTENDED IN ROOMS

52 CAMBRIDGE STREET
SW1V 4QQ
ARTISTRESIDENCE.CO.UK
@ARTISTRESIDENCE

GREAT SCOTLAND YARD HOTEL
WESTMINSTER

Every deeply considered detail of this spectacular hotel speaks to London's long and winding history. In the iconic former home of the Metropolitan Police, more than 600 specially commissioned artworks bring the building and its stories to life. The hound-friendly hotel also donates its dog guest fee to a beloved animal welfare charity.

DOG-FRIENDLY DETAILS
FEE: £10 PER NIGHT DONATED TO
BATTERSEA DOGS AND CATS HOME
DOGS UNDER 20KG ALLOWED

3–5 GREAT SCOTLAND YARD
SW1A 2HN
HYATT.COM
@GSY_LONDON

SEA CONTAINERS
SOUTH BANK

Watch the city wake up from your slick room-with-a-view. The location, almost touching the Thames, makes it perfect for early morning river-gazing with your pup in your lap (why yes, that is St. Paul's Cathedral just across the water). Clean lines and a largely black-and-white palette contrast nicely with the slightly nautical feel found across the rest of the Tom Dixon–designed hotel.

DOG-FRIENDLY DETAILS
£100 DEPOSIT PER DOG
DOGS UNDER 10KG ALLOWED
PET WAIVER REQUIRED
DOGS NOT ALLOWED
IN RESTAURANT OR BAR
DOGS MAY NOT BE LEFT
UNATTENDED IN ROOMS

20 UPPER GROUND
SE1 9PD
SEACONTAINERSLONDON.COM
@SEACONTAINERSLDN

THE HARI
BELGRAVIA

Belgravia is a curious mix of prim and proper with total nonchalance. The Hari itself is somewhat the same. Sleek, marble-clad rooms are looked after by expert staff willing to please: they will gladly give you tips for where to window shop on a stroll with your pup. If you are staying back, make the most of the dog-friendly lounge bar and garden terrace.

DOG-FRIENDLY DETAILS
NO ADDITIONAL FEE
ALL DOG SIZES WELCOME
LEAD REQUIRED IN PUBLIC AREAS
DOGS MAY NOT BE LEFT
UNATTENDED IN ROOMS

20 CHESHAM PLACE
SW1X 8HQ
THEHARI.COM
@THEHARILONDON

THE PORTOBELLO HOTEL
NOTTING HILL

The colourful charm of Notting Hill sets the tone for this bohemian boutique hotel. Four-legged guests are welcome in the Roomy Rooms on the lower ground floor. The best bit? Your private courtyard, where you and your dog can hang out in fresh air. As for walks, well, you're in the best spot to sniff out an antique ornament at Portobello Market.

DOG-FRIENDLY DETAILS
FEE: £25 PER PET PER NIGHT
SMALL TO MEDIUM DOGS WELCOME
BED, BOWLS, AND TREATS INCLUDED

22 STANLEY GARDENS
W11 2NG
PORTOBELLOHOTEL.COM
@PORTOBELLOLDN

TREEHOUSE
FITZROVIA

A room with a skyline view comes as standard here. Riffing on the nostalgic allure of a kid's clubhouse, Treehouse rooms feature everything from Paddington Bear to piggy banks and antique globes—and all without feeling ridiculous. Not only are dogs welcome at Treehouse, they'll also enjoy their own mini bar. And if you have a no-dog outing planned, call on the Canine Concierge.

DOG-FRIENDLY DETAILS
CANINE CONCIERGE PROGRAM
DOG-WALKING AVAILABLE
TREATS AVAILABLE
DOGS NOT ALLOWED IN
FOOD AND BEVERAGE AREAS
DOGS MAY NOT BE LEFT
UNATTENDED IN ROOMS

14–15 LANGHAM PLACE
W1B 2QS
TREEHOUSEHOTELS.COM
@STAYTREEHOUSE

<u>EAT</u>

What will it be? A Sunday roast piled with the crispiest
of potatoes, enjoyed with a side of retro board games
and seriously good wine? A humble toastie? Or how about
a boozy brunch followed by spicy chicken in the evening?
When it comes to dining out with your dog, London is here
with the treats—for humans and hounds. Luckily, well-behaved
pups are allowed inside many cafés, restaurants, and pubs—
even the fancy ones—so let the staff indulge them with
strokes, then pop them under the table and sneak them
a scrap—or two.

WATCHHOUSE
MULTIPLE LOCATIONS

With several doors across London, a WatchHouse coffee hop through the city is the perfect way to spend a day with your dog. Start at the Somerset House location, housed in the spectacular Neoclassical building that is home to London's arts centre. Take in your fill of caffeine and culture with a slow-paced wander through its iconic courtyard. From here, make your way to the Thames for an hour-or-so stroll eastward. Crossing at London Bridge, continue on to WatchHouse's flagship to rest and refuel. A generous drink of water for your well-exercised hound, a strong pour-over for you— unless, of course, an espresso martini is in order.

CLOSEST GREEN SPACE
LINCOLN'S INN FIELDS (SOMERSET HOUSE)
POTTERS FIELDS PARK (TOWER BRIDGE)
BERMONDSEY SPA GARDENS (ROASTERY)
ST. MARY'S CHURCHYARD (BERMONDSEY)
FINSBURY CIRCUS GARDEN (ST. MARY AXE)
LINCOLN'S INN FIELDS (FETTER LANE)
ELDER GARDENS (SPITALFIELDS)

—

SOMERSET HOUSE
STRAND
WC2R 1LA

TOWER BRIDGE
37 SHAD THAMES
SE1 2NJ

ROASTERY
36 MALTBY STREET
SE1 3PA

BERMONDSEY
199 BERMONDSEY STREET
SE1 3UW

ST. MARY AXE
70 ST. MARY AXE
EC3A 8BE

FETTER LANE
92 FETTER LANE
EC4A 1EP

SPITALFIELDS
139 COMMERCIAL STREET
E1 6SJ

WATCHHOUSE.COM
@WATCHHOUSE

OTHER NOTEWORTHY COFFEE-TO-GO

If you're seeking great coffee with a dog-friendly feel (of course) to fuel your walks, try these welcoming spots.

ALLPRESS ESPRESSO BAR
SHOREDITCH

58 REDCHURCH STREET
E2 7DP
ALLPRESSESPRESSO.COM
@ALLPRESSESPRESSO

CARAVAN
CLERKENWELL

11–13 EXMOUTH MARKET
EC1R 4QD
CARAVANRESTAURANTS.CO.UK
@CARAVANRESTAURANTS

CLIMPSON & SONS
HACKNEY CENTRAL

67 BROADWAY MARKET
E8 4PH
CLIMPSONANDSONS.COM
@CLIMPSONANDSONS

DAYLESFORD
NOTTING HILL

208–212 WESTBOURNE GROVE
W11 2RH
DAYLESFORD.COM
@DAYLESFORDFARM

FEDERATION COFFEE
BRIXTON

BRIXTON VILLAGE MARKET
UNIT 77-78, COLDHARBOUR LANE
SW9 8PS
FEDERATION.COFFEE
@FEDERATIONCOFFEE

FLAT WHITE
SOHO

17 BERWICK STREET
W1F 0PT
FLATWHITESOHO.CO.UK
@FLATWHITESOHO

GRIND
LONDON BRIDGE

2 LONDON BRIDGE
SE1 9RA
GRIND.CO.UK
@GRIND

HIDDEN COFFEE
CAMDEN

47-49 CAMDEN ROAD
NW1 9SL
SENDCOFFEE.CO.UK
@HIDDENCOFFEECAMDEN

JACOB THE ANGEL
COVENT GARDEN

16A NEAL'S YARD
WC2H 9DP
JACOBTHEANGEL.CO.UK
@JACOBTHEANGELLONDON

KAFFEINE
FITZROVIA

66 GREAT TITCHFIELD STREET
W1W 7QJ
KAFFEINE.CO.UK
@KAFFEINELONDON

MONMOUTH COFFEE COMPANY
BOROUGH

2 PARK STREET
SE1 9AB
MONMOUTHCOFFEE.CO.UK
@MONMOUTHCOFFEE

PRUFROCK
HOLBORN

23–25 LEATHER LANE
EC1N 7TE
PRUFROCKCOFFEE.COM
@PRUFROCKCOFFEE

ROSSLYN
THE CITY

78 QUEEN VICTORIA STREET
EC4N 4SJ
ROSSLYNCOFFEE.COM
@ROSSLYNCOFFEE

TOWPATH
HAGGERSTON

42 DE BEAUVOIR CRESCENT
N1 5SB
TOWPATHLONDON.COM
@TOWPATHLOLO

WORKSHOP
MARYLEBONE

1 BARRETT STREET
W1U 1AX
WORKSHOPCOFFEE.COM
@WORKSHOPCOFFEE

DRINKS

ERDANT BEER   4,5

OLIVER CIDER   4,5

ANCESTRAL WINES

WHITE   LIGHT-MINERAL-DRY

ROSE   VIBRANT-JUICY

RED   LIGHT-CRUNCHY-JUICY

                               5

WOOD FIRED FLAT BREAD

WILD GARLIC BUTTER   5

SMOKED AUBERGINE   5
& WALNUT

GOOD EARTH GROWERS SALAD   5.5

LUNCH   11.

CHEESE CROQUETTE

CORNISH SCA
CHILLI-HONEY-LEMO

ENGLISH AS
EGG MAYONNAISE

GRILLED MU
TURNIPS-BLACK PE

GOATS CURD
COURGETTES-CRUSHE

FISH FINGER

CORNISH FISH G

WHOLE MAC
ROASTED PEPPERS

WHOLE PLA
SMOKED POTATOES

PAVILION CAFÉ
HACKNEY

Top up your stroll around Victoria Park by settling in among the Frenchies, whippets, and dachshunds of East London at this chilled brunch hotspot. Eggs Benedict and other favourites are on the menu, but you're really here for the Sri Lankan breakfast—a bountiful and fragrant plate of moreish hoppers, warming lentil dhal, and flaky roti. Your friend, on the other hand, is here for the homemade dog treats. Pavilion's interiors are flooded with natural light thanks to a vast glass dome, but still, one of the breezy lakeside seats is hard to beat in the summer, especially if you're keen to indulge your pup in a bit of duck-spotting.

CLOSEST GREEN SPACE
VICTORIA PARK

—

OLD FORD ROAD
E9 7DE
PAVILIONBAKERY.COM
@WEARETHEPAVILION

CAROUSEL
FITZROVIA

At its core, Carousel is a celebration of fabulous food, creativity, and community. Self-described hosts of "all round awesome experiences, morning, noon and night", Carousel offers wide-ranging workshops (including but not limited to pasta making, food photography, wine tasting, pickling, a barbecue masterclass—the list goes on), as well as regular themed feasts, exhibitions, and much more. Dine with your dog in the outdoor seating for an 'Italo Disco Brunch'—or whatever's on that day—followed by a digestive stroll through nearby Regent's Park.

CLOSEST GREEN SPACE
REGENT'S PARK
—

**19-23 CHARLOTTE STREET
W1T 1RL
CAROUSEL-LONDON.COM
@CAROUSEL_LDN**

BISTROTHEQUE
BETHNAL GREEN

Treat your well-behaved dog to fine dining with an off-beat edge—like white linens in a warehouse setting—by taking a seat at Bistrotheque, a pioneer of the Bethnal Green food scene. The inked-up front-of-house will be friendly to you and your four-legged guest, while the team on the pans has been plucked from some of the world's most iconic restaurants. Outstanding side dishes of corn gratin and garlicky crushed potatoes nearly outshine velvety steak and delicate fish mains, all from a menu of French classics with a modern twist. The space is lively and fun, particularly when the music is cranked, and wonderfully affordable (go for the three-course prix fixe).

CLOSEST GREEN SPACE
VICTORIA PARK

—

**23–27 WADESON STREET
E2 9DR
BISTROTHEQUE.COM
@BISTROTHEQUE**

26 GRAINS
COVENT GARDEN

Along Neal's Yard—the bustling alley that connects Short's Gardens and Monmouth Street—flowers and greenery spill over from balconies and window frames of blue, green, and orange. This colour and character is absorbed at street level and amplified by brightly painted shopfronts and an electric weekend energy. An unrushed morning wander with your dog through this technicolour slice of Covent Garden is best punctuated with a visit to 26 Grains. With effective simplicity and principles rooted in seasonality, 26 Grains is famous for its breakfast menu. Pull up a streetside chair and prepare to enjoy a delicious toastie or a flavourful porridge, served with a satisfying side of people- and dog-watching.

CLOSEST GREEN SPACE
SOHO SQUARE GARDENS

—

**1 NEAL'S YARD
WC2H 9DP
26GRAINS.COM
@26GRAINS**

MARE STREET MARKET
LONDON FIELDS

Drop in for eggs on toast, leave with
a Victorian antique lamp tucked under
your arm. Although on first glance
Mare Street Market is all about the food
and drink (arrive for brunch, stay for
cocktails), there's plenty more to this
repurposed East London warehouse,
including a vegan nail salon, barber,
record store, flower shop, and small
antiques warehouse stocking cabinets,
lanterns, and chandeliers hand-plucked
from across the globe. There's something
for everyone, including pups.

CLOSEST GREEN SPACE
LONDON FIELDS

—

**NETIL HOUSE
117 MARE STREET
E8 4RU
MARESTREETMARKET.COM
@MARESTREETMARKET**

EAT

NOBLE ROT
BLOOMSBURY

Visit Noble Rot with your dog as your
date and you'll be treated to a semi-
private table tucked away from the
main room in its townhouse digs. But,
happily, you won't miss out on the vibe
of this casually hip wine bar/restaurant.
Try to work your way through the drinks
list that could keep even the most
discerning of wine lovers satisfied.
Which makes sense: Noble Rot also
produces a magazine on the topic, and
published the book *Wine from Another
Galaxy* in 2020. But the food here is
also sublime: seasonal British produce
is cooked with aplomb. That said, Noble
Rot's a prime spot for cosying up with
a late-night cheese board and a glass
of English bubbles.

CLOSEST GREEN SPACE
RUSSELL SQUARE

—

**51 LAMB'S CONDUIT STREET
WC1N 3NB**
NOBLEROT.CO.UK
@NOBLEROTBAR

OTHER NOTEWORTHY
CASUAL DINING

COLBERT
CHELSEA

Some of West London's finest canines
congregate at this chic restaurant
drawing inspiration from Paris's
effortless boulevard cafés. The outside
tables, overlooking Sloane Square,
are where you want to be for people-
watching while indulging in French
classics with your dog by your side.

50-52 SLOANE SQUARE
SW1W 8AX
COLBERTCHELSEA.COM
@COLBERTCHELSEA

KUDU
PECKHAM

For South African-inspired eats
in South London, treat your dog to
some biltong at stylish Kudu. Work your
way through the menu and relax with
a heady Smokey Kudu (or two). Even
the bread and melted smoked-bacon
butter will knock your paws off. Expect
nothing less from this husband-and-
wife team with hospitality pedigree.

119 QUEEN'S RD
SE15 2EZ
KUDUCOLLECTIVE.COM
@KUDURESTAURANT

ROCHELLE CANTEEN
SHOREDITCH

A hyper-seasonal succinct menu
puts a spin on British classics at this
much-celebrated restaurant. The food
is sensational, the service relaxed, and
the setting a stylish mix of Ercol and
crisp-white walls. Settle in with your
pup on the sun-dappled courtyard,
or opt for a window seat when
the weather calls for a feel-good feast.

16 PLAYGROUND GARDENS
E2 7FA
ARNOLDANDHENDERSON.COM
@ROCHELLECANTEEN

CASA DO FRANGO
LONDON BRIDGE

Lip-tingling chicken grilled in a secret
spicy piri-piri sauce until the skin
is beautifully bronzed makes Casa
do Frango's patrons—including the
four-legged kind—some of the most
committed in town. The spirited team
at this punchy Portuguese spot are dog
lovers through and through—they'll
stop by for strokes as dog eagerly waits
to snuffle up a flaky piece of pastry
from your pastel de nata.

32 SOUTHWARK STREET
SE1 1TU
CASADOFRANGO.CO.UK
@CASADOFRANGO_LONDON

THE BULL AND LAST
HIGHGATE

Back in the 18th century, the last coachstop out of London, before heading north, was at an inn called the Bull—a cry of "the Bull and last" was the signal. That's the name taken by this fine restaurant and boutique inn (note: dogs are only permitted in the pub area), which attracts the hounds and humans from all over London stomping across the nearby Heath. The casual, light-filled space makes an ideal weekend hangout, and they've got enough British ciders and craft ales on tap to make you linger. When you do, take advantage of the kitchen, where they turn out perfectly updated British classics, like homemade Scotch eggs. They'll take care of your pup, too. The Bull and Last's cookbook includes a chapter of recipes dedicated to our four-legged friends.

CLOSEST GREEN SPACE
HAMPSTEAD HEATH
—

168 HIGHGATE ROAD
NW5 1QS
THEBULLANDLAST.CO.UK
@THEBULLANDLAST

THE BULL & LAST.

COOKBOOK £50

TOTE BAG £25
NATURAL OR HUNTER GREEN

ASK STAFF FOR DETAILS

THE CULPEPER
SHOREDITCH

The Culpeper's attraction isn't just a trail-blazing chef team who are responsible for some of London's best pub food. The late licence in the ground-floor pub, complete with exposed concrete walls and trailing plants, means the place fizzes with fun until the early hours on the weekend—plenty of time to truly appreciate the long drinks list, including natural wines sourced from small growers across the globe, while pup snoozes on your lap. Go up to the roof terrace, which doubles as an urban garden, and perch with your pup among the herbs and spices that will later be crushed into your cocktails, all while soaking up the cityscape.

CLOSEST GREEN SPACE
ALTAB ALI PARK
—

**40 COMMERCIAL STREET
E1 6LP
THECULPEPER.COM
@THECULPEPER**

OTHER NOTEWORTHY PUBS

THE CLAPTON HART
CLAPTON

Pubs have occupied the site of the Clapton Hart since 1722, but it's only today that this formerly gritty British boozer's popularity has really soared. This is partly thanks to a tented outside garden festooned in string lights, making it a favourite summer hangout. Creative types from the neighbourhood and beyond flock here in colder months for a Sunday roast under the soaring ceilings. Grab a pint of locally brewed pale ale and a flaky sausage roll if you stop in… and one for the dog, too. (A sausage, that is!)

CLOSEST GREEN SPACE
HACKNEY MARSHES

231 LOWER CLAPTON ROAD
E5 8EG
CLAPTONHART.COM
@CLAPTONHARTPUB

THE DRAPERS ARMS
ISLINGTON

Londoners criss-cross the city just to devour this neighbourhood restaurant's Sunday lunch, and who can blame them? The sharing platter, with its hunks of beef and oversized Yorkshires, is one of the best in the capital. Pups are permitted throughout, from the cosy ground floor pub, which is stacked with board games and scattered with candlelit tables, to the spacious upstairs dining room. Start with a tongue-tingling bloody Mary, which will quickly dust off last night's revelries, and loosen your belt a notch for one of their decadent desserts—which go big on rich, dark chocolate.

CLOSEST GREEN SPACE
HIGHBURY FIELDS

44 BARNSBURY STREET
N1 1ER
THEDRAPERSARMS.COM
@THEDRAPERSARMS

THE FLASK
HIGHGATE

Many a playwright and poet have called Highgate—once a little village on the outskirts of London—home. The Flask, on the Heath's edge, has an equally rich history (the oldest part of the building dates back to the 17th century). Today, it's still all cosy nooks and low beams, ready for long afternoons of hearty stews, British ales, and board games with your dog by your side, while the flower-filled garden is designed for shandies and spritzes. If you're on your way to trample the Heath, this is a prime pit stop.

CLOSEST GREEN SPACE
HAMPSTEAD HEATH

77 HIGHGATE WEST HILL
N6 6BU
THEFLASKHIGHGATE.COM
@THE.FLASK.N6

THE MARKSMAN
HAGGERSTON

Brilliant British food served in a casually elegant pub has earned the Marksman, from St. John alumni Tom Harris and Jon Rotheram, its cult-like status. Opt for a roast and you'll have some of the finest beef titbits your dog has ever had the good fortune to try. During the week, rich pies, beef and barley buns with horseradish (the house speciality), and creamy puddings highlight why foodies flock here. Friendly staff will venture out from behind the mahogany bar just to give your dog some well-deserved fuss, and a biscuit or two.

CLOSEST GREEN SPACE
HAGGERSTON PARK

254 HACKNEY ROAD
E2 7SJ
MARKSMANPUBLICHOUSE.COM
@MARKSMAN_PUB

THE ORANGE
BELGRAVIA

The Orange adapts to the day—and the hour. Think open fires and big roast platters on Sundays, wood-fired pizzas with a glass of red on weekday evenings, and classic cocktails on the weekends. The cosy dog-friendly ground floor, all statement fireplaces, antique furniture, and plants, will welcome you and your furry sidekick. Come summer, beautifully preened punters spill out onto the street quaffing spritzes and goblets of G&T.

CLOSEST GREEN SPACE
BATTERSEA PARK

37-39 PIMLICO ROAD
SW1W 8NE
THEORANGE.CO.UK
@THEORANGEPUBLICHOUSE

LILY VANILLI BAKERY
BETHNAL GREEN

Baking is an art form. The cakes of Lily Vanilli will attest; each is a brightly coloured, meticulously crafted feast for both eyes and belly. A small east London bakery with a global reputation, Lily Vanilli opened in 2010. Lengthy queues have been a permanent fixture since, but one bite of a vegan brownie, famed sausage roll, or perfectly flaky pastry confirms any wait is worth it. Plus, you'll have company. Lily Vanilli is more than just dog-friendly: it serves Jude's plant-based ice cream for dogs. And the icing on that cake? Jude's donates a portion of proceeds to Battersea Dogs and Cats Home, an organisation that has been rescuing and rehoming animals since 1860.

CLOSEST GREEN SPACE
HAGGERSTON PARK
—

THE COURTYARD, 18 EZRA STREET
E2 7RH
LILYVANILLI.COM
@ LILY_VANILLI_CAKE

OTHER NOTEWORTHY SWEET SPOTS

BREAD AHEAD
MULTIPLE LOCATIONS

Fresh sourdough, brioche buns, custard tarts, and gluten-free options for days—Bread Ahead is what dreams are made of. Arrive early at dog-friendly Borough Market to snaffle the bakery's city-famous doughnuts.

BOROUGH MARKET
CATHEDRAL STREET
SE1 9DE

BREADAHEAD.COM
@BREADAHEADBAKERY

GELUPO
SOHO

Stellar gelato made fresh daily using premium-quality ingredients. Flavours like kiwi, gin, and ricotta compete for your affections with peanut butter stracciatella and bitter chocolate. Once the hard part's over, heaped cone in hand, enjoy a stroll to Green Park with your hound.

7 ARCHER STREET
W1D 7AU
GELUPO.COM
@GELUPOGELATO

LONGBOYS
KING'S CROSS

Made with less sugar than your average treat, Longboys are doughnuts done differently. Choose from fillings such as banoffee and pandan coconut (with help from your hound, who's welcome inside), pair with a coffee, and then cruise with your dog to nearby Regent's Canal.

119 LOWER STABLE STREET
COAL DROPS YARD
N1C 4DR
LONGBOYS.CO.UK
@LONGBOYS_UK

THE DUSTY KNUCKLE
DALSTON

A social enterprise bakery in the heart of Dalston, where dogs are welcome, sandwiches are huge, and hearts are full. Here, young offenders are trained up to become professional bakers, and regular donations of bread and pastries are made to London's frontline workers.

ABBOT STREET
E8 3DP
THEDUSTYKNUCKLE.COM
@THEDUSTYKNUCKLE

FORZA WINE
PECKHAM

With a frozen negroni in one hand, a world-class toastie (yes, they exist) in the other, and a panoramic view of Peckham and beyond—the setting could hardly get better, right? Oh, but it can. Because by your side at Forza Wine sits your hound, undoubtedly delighted to accompany you on a day out to one of London's best rooftop offerings. A retractable glass wall offers floor-to-ceiling views in any season, and, when open, space to spill out onto the generous outdoor dog-friendly deck. Each item on the menu of uncomplicated Italian fare pairs perfectly with its list of Italian-only wines. Come for lazy afternoons several storeys above street level; stay for delicious food and canine company.

CLOSEST GREEN SPACE
PECKHAM RYE PARK AND COMMON
—
THE ROOFTOP
133A RYE LANE
SE15 4BQ
FORZAWINE.COM
@FORZAWINE

OTHER NOTEWORTHY DRINKING HOLES

BOURNE & HOLLINGSWORTH
CLERKENWELL

An elegant assemblage of lust-worthy interiors set the scene in this historic building. There are seven spaces inside the self-dubbed clubhouse— including a greenhouse. Head to the dog-friendly bar, where you're greeted by a glorious marble countertop and mirrored backdrop. It's a place to sink into an armchair and sip on a cocktail with your companion at your heels.

42 NORTHAMPTON ROAD
EC1R 0HU
BANDHBUILDINGS.COM
@BOURNEANDHOLLINGSWORTH

SAGER+WILDE
BETHNAL GREEN

Framed by the proud railway arches of Bethnal Green and overlooking the cobbled stretch of Paradise Row, enjoy a delicious brunch or dinner on the dog-friendly terrace. Work your way through a menu that leans Italian, complemented by a flawless, expertly curated wine list.

250 PARADISE ROW
E2 9LE
SAGERANDWILDE.COM
@SAGERANDWILDE

VINORAMICA BAR
HIGHAMS PARK

A warm and welcoming, dog-friendly neighbourhood wine store specialising in smaller production wines and craft beers. Take your time exploring with your pup at your side, aided by wildly knowledgeable staff, if you need them. Across the road, Vino Tap wine bar welcomes evening walk-ins.

9B THE BROADWAY
E4 9LQ
VINORAMICA.COM
@VINORAMICA_TAP

40FT BREWERY
DALSTON

Three beer-loving friends with a penchant for homebrewing transformed a disused car park into a shipping-container brewery. Now a much-loved haunt of the Dalston community—and their dogs, of course—40FT shares its sprawling beer garden with neighbouring businesses, including a bakery and natural-wine bar.

2-3 ABBOT STREET
E8 3DP
40FTBREWERY.COM
@40FTBREWERY

WRIGHT BROTHERS
BOROUGH MARKET

Tucked among the legendary traders in Borough Market, Wright Brothers serves up freshly caught seafood— much of it responsibly sourced from around the UK—in an intimate, informal space at moderate prices. Co-founders (and brothers-in-law) Ben and Robin decided to leave their careers behind to start slinging oysters back in 2002, after an inspiring trip to an oyster farm in France. That set the ball rolling for what they've created today: two restaurants, a home-delivery offering, and the trust of the city's top chefs. Go straight to the source and book a table outside at Wright Brothers, where pup can join in too.

CLOSEST GREEN SPACE
POTTERS FIELDS PARK

—

BOROUGH MARKET
11 STONEY STREET
SE1 9AD
THEWRIGHTBROTHERS.CO.UK
@WRIGHTBROSLTD

OTHER NOTEWORTHY
FOOD MARKETS

MALTBY STREET MARKET
BERMONDSEY

Tucked away in railway arches, stalwart vendors and plucky start-ups offer mouth-watering plates from every corner of the globe. Fresh-pressed waffles, juicy hunks of bavette steak, cheesy arepas, wood-fired pizzas, triple-cooked duck fat chips—you get the picture: you and your hound best come hungry.

ROPEWALK, MALTBY STREET
SE1 3PA
MALTBY.ST
@MALTBYSTMARKET

MERCATO METROPOLITANO
ELEPHANT AND CASTLE
AND MAYFAIR

Both a market and a community movement towards a more sustainable future, housed in a former paper mill with no single-use plastic in sight. Pull up a seat with your dog at communal tables to enjoy cheese, pizza, and coffee that celebrates local, sustainability-minded makers and growers.

ELEPHANT AND CASTLE
42 NEWINGTON CAUSEWAY
SE1 6DR

MAYFAIR
ST. MARK'S, NORTH AUDLEY STREET
W1K 6ZA

MERCATOMETROPOLITANO.COM
@MERCATOMETROPOLITANO

OLD SPITALFIELDS MARKET
SPITALFIELDS

Deciding what to eat and where to sit is a serious business at this dog-friendly market. Try a juicy pulled pork bagel or a plate of traditional Jamaican fare, chased with a serve of Japanese soufflé pancakes. If the sun is shining, sprawl and feast on the steps of Christ Church.

16 HORNER SQUARE
E1 6EW
OLDSPITALFIELDSMARKET.COM
@OLDSPITALFIELDSMARKET

POP BRIXTON
BRIXTON

Railing against the High Street domination of big-name brands, Pop Brixton is a buzzing hub of creativity home to 55 independent businesses that spill out from shipping containers and into the street. Come with your dog for delicious street food, beer, cocktails, music, and art.

49 BRIXTON STATION ROAD
SW9 8PQ
POPBRIXTON.ORG
@POPBRIXTON

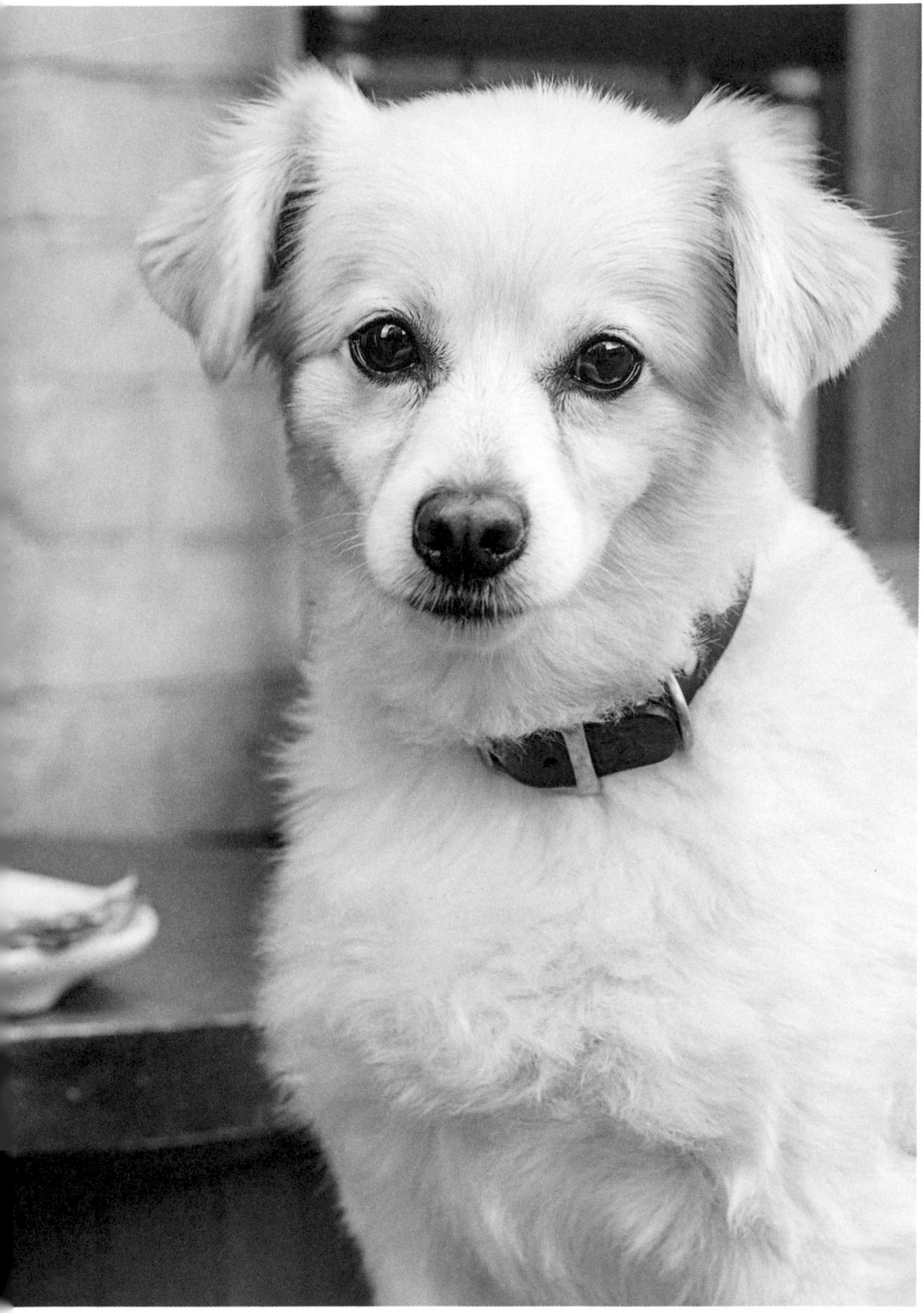

LOOK

In London, four-legged friends aren't relegated to standing outside, gazing up at majestic buildings (although there's plenty of that, too). This city will happily let dogs tour a swanky art gallery, weave between tables full of antiques, or sniff every succulent at your favourite plant shop. Everyone's welcome to have a look, and whether you're in the mood for a shopping spree or simply seeking some quiet inspiration from local artists, you won't be short of choice and culture.

LOVE MY HUMAN
BOUTIQUE AND TOWNHOUSE
CHELSEA

Jenny Matthews merged her two loves, Tibetan terriers and design, to create Love My Human, a Chelsea boutique and dog-grooming salon. Pups can enjoy a blissfully meditative bath while you browse a range of pet accessories, each hand-picked for its quality, functionality, and affordability. Once your pooch is pampered, stop by the LMH townhouse next door. There's a café you can enjoy together, as well as a crèche where you can leave your dog in capable hands for an afternoon.

CLOSEST GREEN SPACE
BATTERSEA PARK
—
308 KING'S ROAD
SW3 5UH
LOVEMYHUMAN.CO.UK
@LOVE.MY.HUMAN

NOTEWORTHY
DOG LABELS

KINTAILS

To founder Genesta Gunn, who knows her way to canine hearts well, dogs are both the driving force and a main source of inspiration. Kintails works with local artisans to responsibly produce small quantities of stylish leather goods, ceramic bowls, fleece jackets, and more.

KINTAILS.COM
@KIN_TAILS

HINDQUARTERS

Founded by Alex Sullivan and Jeremy Cooper, Hindquarters makes sturdy dog beds, bowls, leads, and collars in factories and workshops all over the UK. Their signature slot-and-lock collars are both clever feats of engineering and things of beauty.

HINDQUARTERS.COM
@HINDQUARTERS_HQ

MUNGO & MAUD

Mungo & Maud have been the go-to purveyors for well-heeled pups since 2005. The Sloane Square shop celebrates all aspects of dog-dom, with toys, treats, and essentials for every occasion—even the 'mishaps'.

MUNGOANDMAUD.COM
@MUNGOANDMAUD

OCCAM

With their elongated bodies, sighthounds are often overlooked when it comes to standard-size attire. Enter Occam, which caters to these beautiful canines with perfect-fitting jumpers, coats, and onesies handmade in London.

OCCAMSTORES.COM
@OCCAMSTORES

VACKERTASS SUPPLY CO.

If your dog digs Scandinavian minimalism, east London lifestyle brand Vackertass Supply Co. has your pup covered. Simple leather-and-brass leads and harnesses are designed to soften over time and mould to your furry pal's unique physique.

VACKERTASS.CO
@VACKERTASSSUPPLYCO

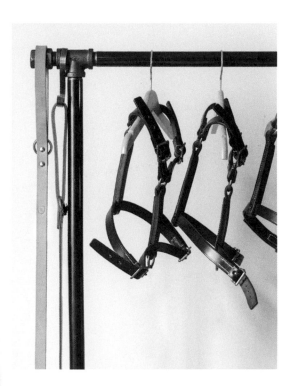

SOMERSET HOUSE
HOLBORN

The former home of queens, architects, and—whisper it—the Inland Revenue, Somerset House is one of London's most celebrated and beautiful cultural spaces. A roster of events, from music to outdoor cinema screenings, takes place here, but really the simplest pleasure is sipping a coffee outdoors with your pup while appreciating this Neoclassical architectural masterpiece. Even if, with pup in tow, you can't pop inside to explore the exhibitions and galleries, a visit is still wholly worthwhile. Much of the joy is in its huge 18th-century courtyard. This serene, sun-soaked South Bank hangout feels like a magical escape in a bustling city.

CLOSEST GREEN SPACE
VICTORIA EMBANKMENT GARDENS
—

STRAND
WC2R 1LA
SOMERSETHOUSE.ORG.UK
@SOMERSETHOUSE

DAVID ZWIRNER
MAYFAIR

Tucked behind the white-washed façade of a Georgian townhouse in Mayfair you'll find one of the most extraordinary of contemporary galleries. Well-behaved small dogs on leads are free to walk by your side as you enjoy the three gallery floors, which have seen the works of Belgian visual artist Luc Tuymans, famed for exploring people's relationship with history, and wire sculptures of the hugely revered American artist Ruth Asawa. With outposts in Hong Kong, New York, and Paris, and a podcast to tap into no matter where you are, David Zwirner isn't only a place to see high-end art; it creates a space for contemplation and uses the medium to shift perspectives.

CLOSEST GREEN SPACE
GREEN PARK
—

**24 GRAFTON STREET
W1S 4EZ
DAVIDZWIRNER.COM
@DAVIDZWIRNER**

SERPENTINE PAVILION
HYDE PARK

Each summer the Serpentine Gallery gives over its outdoor pavilion to an internationally acclaimed architect. The huge structures, handily located in Kensington Gardens from June to October, have become a meeting place for some of the city's most cultured pedigrees. Sure, your hound may not appreciate the talent behind each year's vision, with the likes of Sou Fujimoto and Zaha Hadid being just two of the architects to showcase their work here since it began in 2000, but even novice design enthusiasts will appreciate summer's most sought-out marvel.

CLOSEST GREEN SPACE
KENSINGTON GARDENS
—

DOGS SHOULD BE KEPT
ON A LEAD INSIDE THE PAVILION
**W2 3XA
SERPENTINEGALLERIES.ORG
@SERPENTINEUK**

MODERN ART
CLERKENWELL
AND MAYFAIR

There's a relaxed vibe in both
of Modern Art's outposts: a converted
5,000-square-foot pre-war factory
building in Clerkenwell, and a smaller,
but no less worthy, space in the heart
of Mayfair. Both happily welcome
dogs on leads, leaving you to stroll
around the pristine white spaces and
their roster of exhibitions together—
up to 14 a year, no less. Major artists
are represented here, including Richard
Tuttle and Jacqueline Humphries,
but you're just as likely to enjoy the
work of the new artists. With art-loving
pup Willo by his side, founder Stuart
Shave assists artists in the development
of their practice and creation of
new work.

CLOSEST GREEN SPACE
ST. LUKE'S GARDEN (CLERKENWELL)
GREEN PARK (MAYFAIR)

—

CLERKENWELL
4-8 HELMET ROW
EC1V 3QJ

MAYFAIR
7 BURY STREET
SW1Y 6AL

MODERNART.NET
@STUARTSHAVEMODERNART

OTHER NOTEWORTHY
ART SPACES

ALISON JACQUES
FITZROVIA

Leading the way for overlooked
contemporary artists—with a focus
on women—is Alison Jacques.
The curator's expert eye is only
matched by a passion for her work,
and the works on her gallery walls
are industry-shifting.

16-18 BERNERS STREET
W1T 3LN
ALISONJACQUES.COM
@ALISONJACQUESGALLERY

COPELAND PARK &
BUSSEY BUILDING
PECKHAM

Take your dog for a spin through the
galleries, workshops, and studios at
this community-driven cultural hub
in the heart of Peckham. The industrial
building is also home to a rooftop bar
offering painterly views of London.

133 COPELAND ROAD
SE15 3SN
COPELANDPARK.COM
@COPELANDPARKSE

FLOWERS
SOHO

The Flowers family (including pup
Lillie) has been touting international
art from an eponymous space since
1971. The gallery has seen a few
locations across London—it was one
of the first to open in Shoreditch—
but no matter where, it's always worth
seeing what's on.

DOGS MUST BE KEPT ON A LEAD
21 CORK STREET
W1S 3LZ
FLOWERSGALLERY.COM
@FLOWERSGALLERY

HANNAH BARRY
PECKHAM

Like with her pioneering non-profit
Bold Tendencies, Hannah Barry's
namesake gallery places a strong
emphasis on experimentation, and
encourages a roster of international
artists to take risks in their work.

DOGS MUST BE KEPT ON A LEAD
4 HOLLY GROVE
SE15 5DF
HANNAHBARRY.COM
@HANNAHBARRYGALLERY

ARTWORK FEATURED BY SANYA KANTAROVSKY.
COURTESY OF THE ARTIST AND MODERN ART, LONDON.

DOG-FRIENDLY LONDON **111**

LIBRERIA
SPITALFIELDS

Designed by Spanish architects SelgasCano, Libreria is an east London treasure trove of wall-to-wall, floor-to-ceiling books. Titles are organised loosely by themes such as 'wanderlust' and 'the city', making for eventful searching no matter what you're looking for. Think of Libreria as the paper-bound antidote to 'recommended titles' algorithms. So much so that it's a digital-free space. Tuck your phone away and enjoy the all-too-rare, mind-quieting sanctuary of screen-free time in one of the nooks, with your pup by your side. Browsing around calls to mind the words of Jorge Luis Borges (whose short story *The Library of Babel* inspired the store's interior): "I've always imagined that Paradise will be a kind of library." And this particular paradise is dog-friendly.

CLOSEST GREEN SPACE
WEAVERS FIELDS
—
65 HANBURY STREET
E1 5JP
LIBRERIA.IO
@LIBRERIALONDON

OTHER NOTEWORTHY BOOKSTORES

ARTWORDS
MULTIPLE LOCATIONS

It's impossible to walk past Artwords and not want to go in. The magazine- and book-filled windows are just the jumping-off point for the stacks of printed pages inside dedicated to creativity and visual arts. Check @barkwords, Artword's IG account celebrating four-legged customers.

LONDON FIELDS
20-22 BROADWAY MARKET
E8 4QJ
ARTWORDS.CO.UK
@ARTWORDSBOOKSHOP

DAUNT BOOKS
MULTIPLE LOCATIONS

It's rare to find a bookstore as elegant as Daunt Books Marylebone, and even more unusual that you can browse the beautiful shelves with your hound at your heels. The Edwardian outpost is flanked in old oak and bright skylights. Plan to linger.

MARYLEBONE
83-84 MARYLEBONE HIGH STREET
W1U 4QW
DAUNTBOOKS.CO.UK
@DAUNTBOOKS

JOHN SANDOE BOOKS
CHELSEA

Independently run since 1957, John Sandoe Books is a Chelsea institution spread across three floors of an 18th-century building. The massive store stocks thousands of books but will track down any copy you can't find here, like that one you-know-who chewed up.

10-12 BLACKLANDS TERRACE
SW3 2SR
JOHNSANDOE.COM
@JOHNSANDOEBOOKS

THE SECOND SHELF
COVENT GARDEN

You can't miss the Second Shelf's bright red façade, but even in beige it would still stand out for its dedication to rediscovering works by women. Everyone is welcome inside this cosy, wallpaper-lined space—even dogs.

14 SMITH'S COURT
W1D 7DW
THESECONDSHELF.COM
@SECONDSHELFBOOKS

UNTO THIS LAST
HERNE HILL AND SHOREDITCH

The team at Unto This Last believe that their working environment should be as elegant as the products they craft within it. The upshot? Two of the city's most beautiful workshops. Pop by the Herne Hill location in the south or Brick Lane in the east and you'll have the rare chance to witness the creative process up close. Shelves, sofas, and stools are each lovingly crafted from simple and sustainable birch plywood, and bright-white walls are neatly lined with tools. Products range from wooden children's toys to stylish armchairs— the perfect purchase for your dog's next snooze spot.

CLOSEST GREEN SPACE
BROCKWELL PARK (HERNE HILL)
BOUNDARY GARDENS (SHOREDITCH)

—

HERNE HILL
2–6 HALF MOON LANE
SE24 9HU

SHOREDITCH
230 BRICK LANE
E2 7EB

UNTOTHISLAST.CO.UK
@UNTOTHISLAST_WORKSHOP

EARL OF EAST
HACKNEY AND KING'S CROSS

On a backstreet of Hackney, follow your
nose to Earl of East, purveyor of fine
fragrances and assorted beautiful objects.
The dog-friendly store is best known
for its signature hand-poured candles,
complemented by a tightly curated
range of homewares, books, plants, and
apparel. In Coal Drops Yard, a second,
larger space plays host to workshops.
Browse with your hound (who'll likely be
transfixed by the store's resident French
bulldog, Piper) before enjoying a leisurely
amble through the surrounding Arup-
designed shopping and dining district.

CLOSEST GREEN SPACE
LONDON FIELDS (HACKNEY)
SAINT PANCRAS GARDENS (KING'S CROSS)
—
HACKNEY
5A GRANSDEN AVENUE
E8 3QA
KING'S CROSS
87 COAL DROPS YARD
N1C 4DQ
EARLOFEAST.COM
@EARLOFEAST

KIOSKAFÉ
PADDINGTON

Few things pair as perfectly as
good coffee and the morning paper.
Monocle's Kioskafé celebrates these
simple pleasures in the publication's
signature style. An elegant protest
against the notion that print is dead,
the clean, cool and minimal space
is home to more than 300 impeccably
stacked periodicals and both local and
international magazines. Coffee in hand,
newspaper unfurled, hound by your
side, Kioskafé is a conduit to the world
beyond and its boundless stories.
And for stationery enthusiasts,
it's handy to note the compact corner
café also sells journals, cardholders,
and magazine pouches.

CLOSEST GREEN SPACE
HYDE PARK
—
31 NORFOLK PLACE
W2 1QH
KIOSKAFE.COM

BLUE MOUNTAIN SCHOOL
SHOREDITCH

Occupying a corner plot off Brick Lane, the silvery-grey exterior of Blue Mountain School often begs the question: what is this? Step inside the canine-friendly townhouse, ruled by resident Frenchie Brutus, and the answers are slowly revealed. As you explore six floors scented with sweet, healing palo santo, you go from first impressions—it appears to be a gallery, such is the carefully considered layout of the items on display—but in fact it's a shop filled with some of the world's most exquisitely crafted objects. A ceramic ornament, a lovingly tailored Hostem shirt (James Brown and Christie Fels of Hostem are Blue Mountain's founders), and a candle—it's all given room for appreciation.

CLOSEST GREEN SPACE
WEAVERS FIELDS
—

9 CHANCE STREET
E2 7JB
BLUEMOUNTAIN.SCHOOL
@BLUEMOUNTAINSCHOOL

OTHER NOTEWORTHY SPECIALTY STORES

SCP
SHOREDITCH

Sheridan Coakley has been putting modern British design—and Shoreditch itself—on the global map since launching SCP on Curtain Road in 1985. Drop in to this shop-turned-showroom and take home a pup-approved sofa or display-worthy homewares.

135–139 CURTAIN ROAD
EC2A 3BX
SCP.CO.UK
@SCPLTD

LABOUR AND WAIT
MULTIPLE LOCATIONS

For slow living at its finest, head to this shop stocking lust-worthy utilitarian essentials. You'll drool over handcrafted tools, spools of twine, or a Japanese apron, while your pooch hopes you pick up a tin of Beautiful Joe's ethical dog treats.

MARYLEBONE
48 DORSET STREET
W1U 7NE

SHOREDITCH
85 REDCHURCH STREET
E2 7DJ

LABOURANDWAIT.CO.UK
@LABOURANDWAIT

THE NEW CRAFTSMEN
MAYFAIR

Just steps from Hyde Park is the New Craftsmen, a gallery-like shop that gives British and Irish makers a platform for their craft. The mix of artisans all share in attention to detail, focus on form, and commitment to quality.

34 NORTH ROW
W1K 6DG
THENEWCRAFTSMEN.COM
@THENEWCRAFTSMEN

MAGCULTURE
CLERKENWELL

If you live for the latest issue of many a niche magazine, MagCulture is your mecca. Grab your hound and stop in to see what's happening in the world of print; over 600 mags are dedicated to all kinds of topics, each passionately produced.

270 ST. JOHN STREET
EC1V 4PE
MAGCULTURE.COM
@MAGCULTURE

CONSERVATORY ARCHIVES
BETHNAL GREEN

Conservatory Archives is a botanical wonderland in east London's urban core. It's a solid go-to not only for plant purchases, but also for the team's incredible wisdom on how to help our leafy friends live their best lives. You'll find a mish-mash of greenery cocooned within the small Hackney Road shop, from rare bonsai trees to cacti and succulents, all artfully arranged on shelves, on tables, and dangling from the ceiling. Let the team guide you on the most dog-friendly plants as well as those that need to be kept out of paw's reach.

CLOSEST GREEN SPACE
VICTORIA PARK (HACKNEY)
HACKNEY DOWNS (LOWER CLAPTON)
—
HACKNEY
493-495 HACKNEY ROAD
E2 9ED
LOWER CLAPTON
3-7 LOWER CLAPTON ROAD
E5 0NS
CONSERVATORYARCHIVES.CO.UK
@CONSERVATORY_ARCHIVES

OTHER NOTEWORTHY PLANT STORES

COLUMBIA ROAD FLOWER MARKET
BETHNAL GREEN

There is perhaps nothing better than strolling through an outdoor flower market on a gorgeous Sunday morning with your dog on the lead. Have a wander through Columbia Road to sniff out a myriad of varieties, with charming Victorian buildings in the backdrop.

COLUMBIA ROAD
E2 7RG
COLUMBIAROAD.INFO
@COLUMBIAROAD

LONDON TERRARIUMS
PECKHAM

Whether you lack a green thumb or need plant life you can keep away from your four-legged houseguest, London Terrariums will help you get 'gardening under glass'. Join a workshop to design your own and you'll meet adorable resident dog Walnut.

106A NEW CROSS ROAD
SE14 5BA
LONDONTERRARIUMS.COM
@LONDONTERRARIUMS

PETERSHAM NURSERIES
RICHMOND

Go for the plants, stay for the food. It's a bit of a hike to this gorgeous garden centre, but not only is this place teeming with nature and run by a family of dog lovers, Petersham's earth-friendly approach in the kitchen has also earned it a Michelin green star for sustainability.

CHURCH LANE
PETERSHAM ROAD
TW10 7AB
PETERSHAMNURSERIES.COM
@PETERSHAMNURSERIES

WILD AT HEART
NOTTING HILL

The beautifully arranged bouquets inside celebrated florist Nikki Tibbles's Notting Hill shop help support stray dogs. Her foundation, Wild at Heart, funds animal welfare projects and finds new homes for pups in need.

222 WESTBOURNE GROVE
W11 2RH
WILDATHEART.COM
@WILDATHEARTHQ

DOG-FRIENDLY PLANTS
Take care when shopping for botanicals; baby's breath, tulips, aloe vera, and several other common plants are toxic to dogs. Always ask for expert advice from the pros.

AWAY

Tillingham

The salty air off the coast of East Sussex is just the tonic for London's everyday bustle. Explore narrow passageways in the medieval town of Rye, where galleries sit shoulder to shoulder with antiques warehouses and independent coffee shops. Stop at tiny shacks serving fresh-caught fish in Dungeness in Kent, sip like the locals at some of England's best boutique wineries, and let hounds bask in a wind-in-the-fur sprint across the vast sweep of sand at Camber beach. Head back to the city re-energised, with a few bottles of wine tucked into your bag.

TOP RIGHT
AND LEFT
Rae

BELOW
River walk from
Rye to Camber

OPPOSITE PAGE
Mermaid Street

PREVIOUS SPREAD
Rye Harbour
Nature Reserve

TOP RIGHT
Tillingham

TOP LEFT
Rye Harbour
Nature Reserve

BELOW
Tillingham

OPPOSITE PAGE
View from
Prospect Cottage,
Dungeness

RYE

WALK

CAMBER SANDS BEACH

Hundreds of dogs gleefully bolt across the golden sand at this five-mile-long beach—which, thanks to its many dunes, is one of the prettiest in the country. Go at low tide for the ultimate runaround, and check signposts during the summer for dog-friendly stretches if you plan on making a day of it.

MAY TO SEPTEMBER
SIGNPOSTED RESTRICTED AREAS APPLY

VISITSOUTHEASTENGLAND.COM
#CAMBERSANDS

RYE HARBOUR NATURE RESERVE

Peaceful pathways skirt the edges of this vast coastal wetland that 4,355 species of plants and animals call home. In summer it's a riot of colour, with red poppies and purple foxgloves lining the grass. Come winter it takes on a raw, wild aesthetic. Both are sublime.

RYE.SUSSEXWILDLIFETRUST.ORG.UK
@RYEHARBOURNR

RIVER WALK FROM RYE TO CAMBER

Start near the train station and follow the River Rother for an hour-long wander past Rye Harbour and along the main Nature Reserve pathway to the beach. Position your pup by the famous Red Roofed Hut for a picture, and duck into bird hides as you go.

RYE.SUSSEXWILDLIFETRUST.ORG.UK
@RYEHARBOURNR

STAY

CABÜ CABINS
ST. MARY'S

With a cool clutch of cabins dotted across rough grassland—all just metres from the sea in St. Mary's Cove—this Romney Marsh stay will give you a real sense of escaping from it all. Laze in a deckchair by the heated pool, pedal along the coast, or stargaze from your Scandi-style cabin.

HOLIDAYS.CABU.CO.UK
@CABUCABINS

THE GALLIVANT

Beach. Sleep. Eat. That's the motto of the Gallivant, located metres away from Camber's golden dunes. There's a Hamptons-esque vibe here, where runarounds on the beach can be followed with a tea or cocktail in the sun-soaked garden. The dog-friendly bar is a standout, with freshly caught fish for supper and DIY bloody Marys at breakfast.

THEGALLIVANT.CO.UK
@THEGALLIVANT

THE STANDARD INN

For full-on cosiness, try one of the dog-friendly rooms that are very handily located a stumble up the stairs from one of Rye's best, and oldest, pubs (it dates back to the 15th century). Exposed beams, woodburning stoves, and freestanding baths add to the hunker-down-and-relax mood.

THESTANDARDINNRYE.CO.UK
@THESTANDARDINNRYE

WHITEHOUSE

Simple, stylish, and seriously delicious, this contemporary café is a big hit on Rye High Street. Upstairs, zingy white guest rooms, many with modern four-poster beds, are perfect for overnight stays. If you and your canine companion don't have time for an overnighter at Whitehouse, at least make time for coffee and cake. Or opt for something more filling: the halloumi hash topped with fried egg and the fancy bacon roll with flatbread and chilli jam are total perfection.

WHITEHOUSERYE.CO.UK
@WHITEHOUSERYE

EAT

DUNGENESS FISH HUT
ROMNEY MARSH

Grab a picnic bench and stuff yourself silly with fresh-caught seafood at this popular seaside shack in Dungeness, Romney Marsh. Lobster and crab rolls are easy on the palate, but the homemade fish cakes are what keep us coming back. One mouthful for you, another for dog.

@DUNGENESSFISHHUT

TILLINGHAM

Whether they're tagging along on a tour, following you around the shop, or lazing at your feet while you scoff crispy mozzarella-laden pizza at the outdoor restaurant, dogs are more than welcome at this vineyard. The resident lurcher, Achilles, is always keen to say hi.

TILLINGHAM.COM
@TILLINGHAMWINES

THE CLAM IN CAMBER

Ham hock and piccalilli, generously layered in homemade focaccia bread, is just one of the sarnies making the Clam in Camber the best in East Sussex. Set back from the beach, a neon pink light in the shape of a clam claims a spot on the wall, and huge slabs of shortbread brownie line the counter. Get one.

@THECLAMINCAMBER

THE FIG

From epic brunches of Mexican eggs and Peruvian corn cakes to relaxed evening meals, this Rye High Street go-to pulls in the best ingredients from local suppliers to give you a true taste of Kent. Tuck your dog under your table or grab a Monmouth coffee to go.

THEFIGRYE.COM
@THEFIGRYE

THE SHIP INN

Sip shandies at a table in the sun or cosy up inside beneath beams wrapped in fairy lights. The Ship Inn dates back to the 16th century, and this local pub doesn't just welcome dogs—it truly adores them.

THESHIPINNRYE.COM
@THESHIPINNRYE

THE YPRES CASTLE INN

Tucked away beneath the ramparts of Rye Castle, this historic pub has a fireplace and beams, but the real lure is the huge grassy garden illuminated in festoon lights. Settle in and work your way through the excellent menu of indie wineries and breweries.

YPRESCASTLEINN.CO.UK
@YPRESCASTLEINN

LOOK

CAMBER CASTLE

The vast ruins of the 16th-century Camber Castle, built by Henry VIII to defend the coast from France, are worth an up-close inspection. Stroll the outside loop walk from Rye town as it follows an old railway track and the river.

ENGLISH-HERITAGE.ORG.UK
@ENGLISHHERITAGE

DEREK JARMAN'S PROSPECT COTTAGE

Set in the otherworldly desert-come-beach landscape of Dungeness in Kent, this black cottage—accented by daffodil-yellow window frames—was owned by artist and filmmaker Derek Jarman before he passed away in 1994. An Art Fund campaign has saved it, while Jarman's sketches can be seen at Tate Britain.

#PROSPECTCOTTAGE

MERMAID STREET

With its pristine white-washed cottages and overflowing flower boxes, it's no surprise that this is one of the most photogenic cobbled streets in the country. The Mermaid Inn, partway down, dates back to the 12th century, and smugglers' tunnels lead from its cellars beneath the streets of the old town.

RYEMUSEUM.CO.UK
#MERMAIDSTREETRYE

THE SOUND MIRRORS

These huge concrete structures (we're talking 20 to 30 feet tall, with one around 200 feet wide) were once used to detect the engine noise of enemy aircraft back in the 1920s and '30s. Head to Greatstone Lakes in the Dungeness Nature Reserve to see them.

THEROMNEYMARSH.NET/
SOUNDMIRRORS
@THEROMNEYMARSH

FETCH

MCCULLY & CRANE

Pups are offered tasty biscuits as they enter this light-filled shop and art gallery, where walls are lined with colourful abstract artworks. The shop's co-owner, Marcus Crane, helped source the lust-worthy antiques and art for the bedrooms of nearby Tillingham Winery.

MCCULLYANDCRANE.COM
@MCCULLYANDCRANE

NIGHTINGALE CIDER
TENTERDEN

Take a small detour to check out a family-run craft cider business. Nightingale Cider is run by Sam and Tim, two siblings whose father has grown the apples and pears that create their fresh, zingy concoctions. The farm shop also stocks locally made chutneys, jams, and more.

NIGHTINGALECIDER.COM
@NIGHTINGALECIDER

PUCKHABER DECORATIVE ANTIQUES

Artfully curated by mother-and-son team Jackie Harris and Martyn Fowler, some of the finest antique furniture in the country is waiting to be admired in this exquisite white-washed shop. Can't cart that floor-length mirror home? Don't worry: shelves are lined with sandalwood-scented washes and lotions from Frama Apothecary.

PUCKHABERDECORATIVE
ANTIQUES.COM
@PUCKHABERDECOR

RAE

Vintage interior pieces and household items lovingly sourced by owner Alexa Shaw, from balms to rugs and soaps to vases, make Rae not just fun to visit, but also a destination. Pop into the store on your way to the beach to meet resident dog Ruby.

RAELIFESTYLE.COM
@RAE_LIFESTYLE_

Amble along pathways once trodden by Romans looking to wallow in steamy waters: Bath wraps the best of a relaxed break into one compact city. With dog in tow, your itinerary can head in various directions, from a hop around town checking out bookstores, art galleries, and cafés serving freshly baked sourdough, to a romp through the bucolic Cotswolds a short drive away. A stay in Bath will make you feel like you're in a Georgian dream. That calls for breakfast in bed, for two.

TOP RIGHT
Năm

TOP LEFT
Royal Crescent

BELOW LEFT
The Beckford
Bottle Shop and Bistro

OPPOSITE PAGE
Năm

TOP RIGHT
Berdoulat

BELOW RIGHT
Pulteney Bridge

OPPOSITE PAGE
Alexandra Park

TOP RIGHT
Magalleria

TOP LEFT
Oak

BELOW LEFT
Society Café

OPPOSITE PAGE
Walcot House

BATH

WALK

ALEXANDRA PARK

It's a calf-quivering hike up— the steeper route is not one for older dogs. But for younger pups, it's worth climbing to the top of Alexandra Park for the best views over the city. Bring a picnic for spring or summer visits, or stomp through burnt-orange leaves come autumn.

VISITBATH.CO.UK
#ALEXANDRAPARKBATH

BATH SKYLINE WALK

Wander through ancient woodland, hopping over stiles and meandering through meadows of wildflowers, on this undulating six-mile route. The Bath Skyline walk stretches across a wide circle in the countryside, around the edge of the city. Yellow National Trust arrows mark the way.

NATIONALTRUST.ORG.UK
#BATHSKYLINEWALK

PRIOR PARK

This immaculately kept 18th-century park combines beautiful Georgian architecture, fascinating history, and large swathes of green grass to stretch out on. The Palladian Bridge, one of only four such bridges in the world, is remarkable. A place to be shared, dogs on lead are welcome.

NATIONALTRUST.ORG.UK
@NTPRIORPARK

THE COTSWOLDS

It's a little further afield, but if you're travelling from London by car, a ramble in the Cotswolds is perfect for breaking up the journey. The 102-mile-long Cotswold Way goes from the charming stone houses in Chipping Campden, through beech woodlands and grassland, and on to the heart of Bath.

COTSWOLDS.COM
@THE_COTSWOLDS

STAY

HARINGTON'S HOTEL

Just a 10-minute walk from Royal Victoria Park, this 13-room boutique hotel welcomes dogs of all sizes. The dog-centric team will happily point you to nearby eateries and recommend adventures suited to your, and your furry friend's, needs, from secluded picnic spots to the best strolls along the Kennet and Avon canal.

HARINGTONSHOTEL.CO.UK
@HARINGTONS_HOTEL

NO.15 GREAT PULTENEY

Marble fireplaces, statement headboards, grand chandeliers. This 37-room hotel, set within a series of townhouses, is one of the plushest pup-friendly stays we've seen, and it feels very much like you're swanning around your own Georgian home. Dogs are so adored that local sitters and walkers are on hand to help.

GUESTHOUSEHOTELS.CO.UK/
NO-15-GREAT-PULTENEY-BATH
@GUESTHOUSEHOTELS

THE ROSEATE VILLA

Why not choose a hotel that offers your pup plenty of room to enjoy, both in and out? Set across two Victorian houses directly across from Henrietta Park, Roseate Villa—and its resident border terrier, Muttley—welcomes your canine partner with a 'woof' box filled with treats from Lily's Kitchen, and a tennis ball. Fetch!

ROSEATEHOTELS.COM
@THEROSEATEVILLABATH

THE ROYAL CRESCENT HOTEL & SPA

Set within one of Bath's main historical landmarks—a row of grand Georgian houses—this elegant spa and hotel is just steps from flower-filled Royal Victoria Park. Six of their elegant bedrooms are dog-friendly, all with direct courtyard access. Dogs can't dine in the restaurant, so wrap up for breakfast on the terrace, or opt to have it in your room.

ROYALCRESCENT.CO.UK
@ROYALCRESCENT_HOTEL

EAT

COLONNA & SMALL'S

Wooden floors and sun streaming through skylights create a relaxed vibe for humans and dogs alike at one of Bath's best coffee spots. Try a brew at the bar and grab a bag of beans to go—they only stock what they absolutely love.

COLONNACOFFEE.COM
@COLONNACOFFEE

LANDRACE BAKERY

Located a little further from the main tourist thoroughfares and all the better for it, this bakery is known for its sourdough bread and loaves made from UK-grown grains. Thursday's sourdough pizza night is a must if you're in town.

LANDRACEBAKERY.COM
@LANDRACEBAKERY

OAK

Many of the vegetables and herbs you'll try at Oak have been grown in the restaurant's own organic garden just outside of Bath. It sets the tone for the ever-evolving plant-based menu, which is built from what's in season and available locally. If you can't stop to eat, at least pick up a bottle or two of natural wine.

OAKRESTAURANT.CO.UK
@OAKRESTAURANTBATH

SOCIETY CAFÉ

Dogs sit hopefully at their human's feet waiting for buttery croissant flakes at this excellent café, which also has plenty of outdoor space. Keen on pastries? Go early—they sell out fast.

SOCIETY-CAFE.COM
@SOCIETYCAFE

WALCOT HOUSE

This indie restaurant and bar is the place to start the day with a pastry and coffee or end it with a relaxed meal and aperitif. Whichever you choose, dogs are always welcome, and there's plenty of space to stretch out or curl up beneath your table—with the occasional spot of fuss from the team.

WALCOTHOUSEBATH.COM
@THEWALCOTBATH

WHITE HART
BATHWICK

A locally distilled gin and tonic in the jasmine-scented garden of the White Hart is hard to beat. On a summer's day, the Mediterranean vibe is irresistible, but if you and your dog are hunkering down at the bar on a cool day, the cosy-casual comfort and seasonal soups are spot on.

WHITEHARTBATH.CO.UK
@WHITEHARTBATH

LOOK

BERDOULAT

Patrick and Neri are the couple behind this store that's named after Patrick's childhood home in France. Each item in the collection is specially selected—many are sourced from local artisans based within an hour's drive of the studio. Visit for ceramics, textiles, and more.

BERDOULAT.CO.UK
@BERDOULAT_INTERIOR_DESIGN

GALLERY NINE

Dogs are free to join you as you browse affordable contemporary ceramics, paintings, and textiles in this indie gallery-come-concept shop on Margaret's Buildings. Beware of excited wagging tails: there are breakables on display.

GALLERYNINEBATH.COM
@GALLERYNINEBATH

GRAY MCA ON MARGARET'S BUILDINGS

Just along from Gallery Nine is the light-filled Gray MCA. The space celebrates the wonders of fashion illustration, modern artist textiles, and design. Check the site for info on upcoming exhibitions.

GRAYMCA.COM
@GRAYMCA

ROYAL CRESCENT

It's impossible to not be impressed by this 538-foot-long crescent of 30 honey-coloured Georgian townhouses, designed by architect John Wood the Younger. They are part of the reason Bath was awarded UNESCO World Heritage status in 1987—one of only 32 sites in the UK.

VISITBATH.CO.UK
#ROYALCRESCENT

SHAM CASTLE

The clue's in the name: this castle masquerades as a medieval fortress but was only built around 300 years ago. A sham castle, of course, but your pup won't sniff out the difference. It's part of the Bath Skyline walk.

NATIONALTRUST.ORG.UK
#BATHSKYLINEWALK

FETCH

ALWAYS SUNDAY

You could lose hours in this laid-back shop, which specialises in finishing touches. Vintage glassware, linen cushion covers, and sequinned tablecloths will really elevate your interiors.

ALWAYSSUNDAY.STORE
@ALWAYS_SUNDAY_STORE

FOUND

From hair clips to handbags, and colourful clothes to stationery, you're sure to find something you love at Found. Pick something up for yourself or as a present for two- or four-legged pals back home.

FOUNDBATH.CO.UK
@FOUNDBATH

MAGALLERIA

Made by print magazine lovers, for print magazine lovers. The world's best indie and specialist mags call Magalleria home. Shop dogs Enzo and Alfie snooze in their beds while you take in the shelves.

STORE.MAGALLERIA.CO.UK
@MAGALLERIABATH

NĀM

If you can't resist sniffing out expensive glass candles—especially those of the heavenly Cire Trudon type—you may need to pass by Nām. But, don't. Founder Sharan Kaur has plenty of special pieces for your home.

@NAMSTORE_BATH

THE BECKFORD BOTTLE SHOP

Floor-to-ceiling bottles of wine, beer, and cider make this one of the best browsing shops in the city. Grab a drink at one of the outdoor tables or pop next door for cheese and charcuterie.

BECKFORDBOTTLESHOP.COM
@BECKFORDBOTTLESHOP

TOPPING & COMPANY

Dogs can sprawl out on the floorboards waiting for biscuits in this relaxed indie bookstore, which doubles as a coffee spot. The staff are true bibliophiles; swing by one of their evening events to celebrate their authors.

TOPPINGBOOKS.CO.UK
@TOPPINGSBATH

DOG
FRIE

NDS

SOPHIE SELLU AND STANLEY

There's an elegance to Sophie Sellu's hand-crafted wooden forms, and at the same time a durability. A slender oak vase stands tall on two bowlegs. A textured walnut brush with Tampico plant fibre bristles has a wave-like wobbled edge. Sophie first discovered the joy of woodcarving as a schoolgirl, and today her one-woman business, Grain & Knot, produces beautiful yet functional objects for the kitchen and home. She works between a dusty brick shed in her garden and a small carving workshop in her spare room. Wherever she is, she's accompanied by Stanley, an affectionate whippet with a silky black coat and a snow-white chest. "I can get quite engrossed in what I'm doing, and he reminds me when it's time to call it a day," she says, smiling. "He gets fed at six o'clock, and he just comes over and stares at me until I put down my tools."

It was while working in fashion that Sophie rediscovered her love of woodwork. After she graduated with a degree in interior design from the Manchester School of Art in 2009, and was made redundant from a visual merchandising job in retail, Sophie found herself doing concept design. Her love of nature and her need to work with her hands was an escape. "I started signing up to lots of creative courses," she says, pinpointing one that sparked a change inside her: a spoon-whittling workshop deep in the British countryside. "I drove down from London at about six in the morning and stayed all day. We built a fire and we learned about trees. It changed things for me."

Spurred into starting her own business, Sophie completed the Prince's Trust Enterprise Scheme and founded Grain & Knot in 2014. She produces six whimsical collections a year and, depending on where she's at in the production cycle, might be sketching and creating cardboard cut-outs or researching and developing ideas. She often works with her boyfriend, also a woodworker, whose family conveniently owns a patch of woodland in Kent. "We usually spend a couple of days a week there, processing timber," she says. Unsurprisingly, Stanley is a big fan. "He's never on the lead when we're there. He just runs around chasing squirrels. If we're working, he'll happily sit under a tree, hanging out with us."

Closer to home in Crystal Palace, Sophie and Stanley take time out in a tiny park around the corner from their house. "We can go out at any time of the day and there will be people to talk to," she says. "It's so nice. If I didn't have him, I'm sure I wouldn't know nearly as many of my neighbours." There's a park WhatsApp group and regular community meetings. "I've suggested that we do something similar to 'The Hounds of Hackney Downs', two mosaics of the local dogs in a park in Hackney. Ours is a nice little park and it's been overlooked by the council, so we're trying to make it better for everyone."

Sophie's hand-hewn pieces make you pay attention to small details that, like her local park, might otherwise go unnoticed. The patterns and grain of timber, which guide the organic shapes of her designs. Smooth and mottled textures. The marks and grooves of her favourite carving knife. Each tactile item is made from either sustainably grown, responsibly sourced, or reclaimed materials; most of the wood Sophie uses comes from storm-damaged trees in Kent. She was inspired to start making vases by the swathes of seemingly useless off-cuts in her garden shed. Everything has potential, nothing is wasted.

Stanley, for one, wouldn't allow it. Sophie has to be careful with what she leaves at his head height. "There have been times when I've left a finished piece out, only to find him chewing it up in his bed," she says. Woodwork can be messy, and it's not uncommon for her to belatedly realise that she's been dragging wood chips around the house in her socks or the turn-ups of her jeans. "Stanley's good, though, and if I've left a piece of wood on the floor it's my own fault, really—I can't blame him."

PLAYGROUND

Crystal Palace Park is great, as is South Norwood Country Park, which isn't too far from us. It's almost like a nature reserve: it's quite overgrown, and there are lots of paths that run through it and a big lake.

LOCAL HANGOUT

Most of the pubs in Crystal Palace are dog-friendly. Bridge House is my local, right by the park, and there's another called Sparrowhawk, which is amazing. I'm desperate to go to Kudu in Peckham, which also welcomes dogs and serves amazing South African food.

AWAY FROM IT ALL

We love going to Camber Sands. It's a lovely place to go for a walk anyway, but Stanley goes absolutely wild, throwing himself around in the sand dunes and digging big holes.

ANDREW TUCK AND MACY

"It's strange when you first start bringing your dog into the office," says *Monocle* editor Andrew Tuck. "You're so aware of everything they do, and you're a bit cautious that they're going to bother people. Then suddenly you realise that having a dog in an office is mostly soothing." Andrew spends his days finding stories, encouraging reporters to dig a little deeper, liaising with the photo and art teams, and bringing everything together on the page in a way that engages and excites readers. With him through it all is his lovable wire-haired fox terrier, Macy, who he's had—"or she's had me, I'm not sure which way round it is"—since 2012. By this point, she too is a regular contributor to the current affairs and lifestyle magazine.

Since it was founded in 2007, *Monocle* has morphed into a global brand, with its own 24-hour radio station, books, films, shops and cafés, and events. "My job is to make sure that all of those things come from the same place and give the audience what they want while also surprising them now and then," says Andrew, who previously worked at the *Independent* and *Time Out*. "To make sure there's a clarity of vision about getting out into the world, being engaged with people, looking after your cities, valuing craft, and trying to deliver quality of life for all in the things you do."

Quality of life that can be improved by walking to work with your dog, for example. Together with his partner, David, Andrew lives in a small but beautifully designed mews house in Bloomsbury (if you're feeling nosy, pick up a copy of *The Monocle Guide to Cosy Homes*). "Although it doesn't have tonnes of room, it has a roof terrace, a nice living space, and it's light and bright," he says. "And you step out of your door and you're in central London." From home, the family of three can be at the British Museum, King's Cross St. Pancras, Smithfield Market, and Covent Garden, all in under 10 minutes.

Andrew and David have been together for more than 30 years and their relationship has been marked by dogs. "When we were first together, he had a border collie cross called Millie, then we had a Weimaraner called Bruno for a decade," says Andrew. "The experience with every dog has been so amazing that we didn't want to repeat it by getting the same breed again." They bought Macy as a puppy after getting the idea of having a fox terrier from some friends. "We went to see the litter—there were two or three puppies—and Macy was incredibly kissy and friendly even as a puppy and we knew that she was the dog for us."

While Andrew was at the *Independent* it wasn't possible for him to take Bruno to work. These days, at *Monocle*, Macy accompanies him to Midori House in London's leafy Marylebone whenever he (or, perhaps, she) wishes. "While she's an independent character in many ways, over time it's transpired that in the office she just wants to know where I am," he says, with a smile. She likes to balance on his lap as he types and curls up by his side on the sofa during editorial meetings: "That's her ideal spot."

As well as being a regular in Midori House, Macy has managed to sneak into the magazine and various book projects, a highlight being a dog-clothing photo shoot with all the office pooches. "She's also popped up as a bit of a prop in a few illustrations," says Andrew. "If you're eagle-eyed, you'll notice that, because she's become such a big part of who I am, the illustration beside my Saturday column for the *Monocle Weekend Edition* often features a fox terrier. And it's the same when I appear in cartoon form in the magazine." All that's left is for Macy's name to make an appearance on the masthead.

PLAYGROUND

Macy is a regular in Regent's Park. She loves playing with other dogs, but she also has moments when she decides enough is enough, especially if the other dog is a puppy. She's eight, so she has a bit of an attitude.

LOCAL HANGOUT

In my neighbourhood there's La Fromagerie, where Macy has curled up under a table on many occasions, and she's also been at the bar of the restaurant over the road, Noble Rot.

FANCY GARB

Macy looks good in clothes, but she has a thick coat and seems to be more affronted than delighted to find herself togged up in too many complicated things. Over the years she's got to know and love Mungo & Maud, though, which has a shop here in London.

NIKKI TIBBLES AND ELLIOT

Since launching Wild at Heart in 1994, Nikki Tibbles has become one of the best-known luxury florists in Britain. Her locally grown blooms can be found in her original Turquoise Island shop in Notting Hill and at the entrance to the iconic department store Liberty London. But Wild at Heart is about more than beautifully arranged bouquets; it also funds the Wild at Heart Foundation, a rescue dog charity Nikki founded in 2015. "I was doing reasonably well with my business, and I love dogs and just wanted to give something back," she says. "So, I decided to set up a charity." There are 600 million stray dogs in our world, none of which are treated justly. Thanks to the foundation, between 50 and 70 dogs are rehomed every month, some to Nikki's own Notting Hill abode.

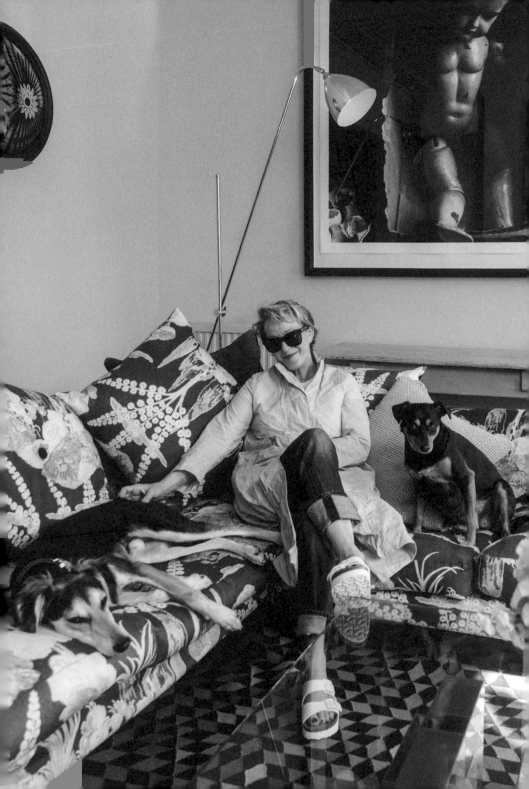

"I'd had dogs all my life, even at university," says Nikki, who was born in Bristol and has lived in London for as long as she can remember. "But I've never bought a bred dog and I never would." At the time of writing, she shares her five-storey home with five large rescues: Lenny the Spanish mastiff, Ronnie the Romanian, Rita and Ruby from Puerto Rico, and the most recent addition to the household, Elliot, a saluki from Bahrain. "I tend to take all the dogs who nobody else wants, which I'm very happy about."

Nikki divides her time between her Notting Hill home and a rural retreat in West Sussex. Wherever she is, she begins and ends her day with a long walk, either at Hampstead Heath or in the South Downs. "Unfortunately, Rita and Ruby are still on Puerto Rico time, so they wake up at about half-past six," she says, laughing. There are no rules in either house; the dogs are welcome to make themselves comfortable on whatever piece of furniture they want, wherever they want. When Nikki's in the city, she always takes two or three into the office with her; if she's working from home, the lot keep her company. "In winter, I lie in front of a fire with all the dogs around me. In fact, I'm often on the floor and they're on the sofa—that's my life."

Since it was founded in 2015, the Wild at Heart Foundation has sponsored rescue projects and awareness campaigns around the world. "The stray dog situation is getting worse and worse, and the only way we'll be able to make ever-lasting change is by change coming from within," says Nikki. "We have to educate, and we have to sterilise. The rehoming element of the charity is the icing on the cake." The foundation works in Romania, Borneo, Cyprus, Greece, and Bosnia, to name a few. "We help wherever we can."

It's on work trips that Nikki often ends up bringing home dogs like Elliot. He and his sister, bred for racing and apparently not quick enough on their toes, were cruelly dumped out in the desert in Bahrain. How does she keep such a motley mix at peace? Newcomers must be introduced gently, away from their home environment. "With the two dogs from Puerto Rico, I would bring one up to London from the country and we'd go for a walk, just one on one, or sometimes I'd take the two new ones with one of the older ones," says Nikki. "It took about six months to integrate them properly."

If it all sounds like a lot of work, that's because it is. But Nikki wouldn't have it any other way. There's always room for one more, too. "I can't imagine living without dogs in my life," she says. "I've grown up with dogs since I was a baby; I used to get up in the middle of the night when I was little and go and sleep with our two boxers downstairs." Today, her five friendly rescue pups accompany her wherever she goes. When she's invited to stay with friends, they know to expect the pack. "They're as big a part of me as anything else in my world."

PLAYGROUND

In London, we go to Hampstead Heath most days. The dogs are generally great with others, though Ronnie the Romanian is quite aloof and prefers to walk beside me on a lead.

LOCAL HANGOUT

Locanda Locatelli is my favourite grown-up restaurant for taking my dogs, and they always bring me a bed and a blanket and a treat, which is wonderful.

AWAY FROM IT ALL

That's my house in Sussex. It's a small property, but it has a big field. Plus, I'm right in the middle of the South Downs.

DUFFY, ELENA SAUREL, AND SUMMER

Head to Victoria Park early enough on a Sunday morning and you might spot a Staffordshire bull terrier gleefully chasing after a bicycle. It's a weekend ritual for east London jeweller Duffy and his pup, Summer. Duffy and his Staffy cycle to the great patch of green from the one-bedroom apartment they share with his partner, the actor and writer Elena Saurel, in Dalston. As soon as he reaches the park's outer fringes, Duffy lifts Summer out of his backpack and the pair do laps. "Then, she has to stop and find the biggest stick she can to tak back to Elena," says Duffy, smiling. "She'll sit with it outside the Ginger Pig butcher, while I pick up some bacon for breakfast, eagerly awaiting the bones they always chuck in."

Summer has been with Duffy and Elena since they started dating. "He got the dog and now I can't leave the relationship," laughs Elena. Unlike Duffy, who was born in Southampton and has been in London most of his life, Elena moved around a bit. The Salvadoran American grew up in Switzerland and Spain before heading to boarding school in the UK, which was followed by acting school in New York. "I didn't have a dog growing up, but I always wanted one," she says. "In fact, my parents promised my sisters, who are 10 years older than me, that they would get a dog when they moved to Switzerland—then my mum fell pregnant and instead they got me."

As if to make up for lost time, Elena not only lives with Summer, but she works with her too. Summer has appeared in a handful of sketches and short films she's made, including *Behind the Mask*, an ongoing ego contest between two male actors. At one point, there's a joke that Elena turns into a dog, and Summer is the dog. "She can be quite the diva," says Elena. "She doesn't like anyone making direct eye contact with her—you can't address her," she laughs. "But yes, she has a lot of on-screen experience."

On-screen and behind the camera, the brindle Staffy is also the star of a jewellery campaign. Duffy hadn't done one before, because so much of his work is commission-based and comes up very quickly, but a good photographer friend offered to do a shoot and Elena helped produce it. "I wanted to shoot my dad, a model friend, my friend's kid, and then the photographer was like, 'How about Summer?' So, we dragged her down here, and she loved it. We put her in loads of bits of expensive jewellery and she'd just wander off around the studio with them."

It's there, at his studio in Shoreditch, that Duffy makes one-of-a-kind fine and precious jewellery. Naturally, Summer has a piece: a solid-silver, hand-engraved necklace. "I'd like to do more dog chains," Duffy says, enthusing about how much fun he had making Summer's. "I like things that are jewellery-related but have a practical purpose. This has her details on it so there's a reason she wears it. I'm not just prettifying my dog."

When they're not working, the trio spend time outside London, at a beach house they're renovating in the small seaside village of Pevensey Bay, between Eastbourne and Hastings. "It's a cool place," says Elena, while describing the beaches and the landscape, and the combination of Art Deco mansions and Edward Scissorhands–style bungalows. "It's kind of Cape Cod meets the UK."

Back in their apartment in Dalston, Summer spends most of her day gazing out of a window that overlooks a buzzy road below. She's happy there, until, that is, Elena starts to put on an accent or a voice while rehearsing or self-recording an audition. "It kind of freaks her out," says Duffy. "She thinks, who is this in the room?" A compliment, then, in a roundabout way, to Elena's acting. Other than that, has having a dog been all it's cracked up to be? Elena doesn't hesitate. "Also, in a slightly selfish way, they just bring so much to your life— the fact that you come home and there's someone who is genuinely so happy to see you all the time, it makes you feel good about yourself."

BEST-KEPT SECRET

Duffy: At the De Beauvoir Arms, there's a lady who has pockets full of dog treats and will overfeed your dog constantly.

Elena: There's also a comedy improv theatre upstairs that has regular shows.

LOCAL HANGOUT

Elena: For a nice dinner there's Bright, which is next to London Fields and does really good food and organic wines. Then there's a wine and tapas place called Weino BIB, whose owner loves dogs.

JADE HARWOOD AND FREDDIE

Just as Jade Harwood's friends were surprised when she told them she wanted to start a knitting revolution, her grandmother was no doubt taken aback when Jade came home one day with a dog the size of her handbag. "My nan used to breed boxers, and I always thought I might end up having that kind of dog one day," she says, as she welcomes Freddie, a miniature dachshund, onto her knee. Jade smiles as she lovingly strokes his tan, smooth-haired ears. Happily, Wool and the Gang, the sustainable fashion brand Jade co-founded in 2008 with fellow fashion student Aurelie Popper and former model Lisa Sabrier, has flourished. And Freddie? Well, he's blossomed, too.

Jade's grandmother not only used to breed boxers, but also taught Jade how to knit. "I was seven at the time, and I used to knit blankets and clothes for my toys," says Jade. "Everything, really." After rediscovering her needles and yarn in her teens, she decided to study textiles at Central Saint Martins, which is where she met Aurelie. The pair teamed up with Lisa and started Wool and the Gang with the mission to make knitting accessible and fun for a younger audience through ready-to-wear clothes, DIY kits, online tutorials, and a global community of knitters. "Knitting used to be a one-to-one experience, generation-to-generation. Through YouTube, any one of us was able to reach millions of people."

After spending four years in New York building the brand, which has collaborated with everyone from Save the Children and the British Fashion Council to And Other Stories and Mini Cooper, Jade returned to London. She and her husband were living on Kingsland Road in Shoreditch, in a small flat suitable for a small dog. Enter Freddie. "Dachshunds are a very practical breed," says Jade, laughing. "He can easily nip around London and, if need-be, squeeze into a bag. Even if a shop doesn't technically allow dogs, I can smuggle him in if I really want to. No one knows he's there because he just hunkers down."

It wasn't long before Freddie snuck into Wool and the Gang too—he was the one who inspired the brand's pet collection, which ranges from a mustard-yellow sleeveless turtleneck to a soft and stretchy bandana, and a sturdy basket for a dog to curl up in. According to Jade, Freddie, who played a big part in the campaign, is a very willing model. "Ever since he was a puppy, he's liked to wear clothes," she says. "He's short-haired, and he weirdly sheds in the winter, so at that time of the year he always wears his jumper."

Freddie is in many ways a typical dachshund. He's friendly but independent. He tolerates other dogs, but he doesn't like puppies. They're too much for him, and he's not afraid to tell them off— or big dogs, for that matter. "He's definitely got a big dog personality," says Jade. "I think he prefers humans, really. He was very popular in our office on Gower Street."

After 12 years with Wool and the Gang, at the end of 2020, Jade stepped down. "During the pandemic I had time to think, and I decided things had come to a natural end," she says, comparing the business to a child leaving home. Right now, she's exploring other ideas and her passion for the environment, working with friends to develop a new housing system that's both sustainable and liveable. That's not to say that she's done with knitting, though. "I'll always be a hardcore crafter. For me, it's a form of meditation and a way to disconnect," she says. "Whenever I'm not working, my favourite way to pass the time is knitting or crocheting in front of the TV, with Freddie cuddled up beside me."

PLAYGROUND
Highams Park is lovely, and then there's Epping Forest. Every time my husband and I go there, I think how lucky we are to have this mega-forest, which feels so ancient and so energising.

LOCAL HANGOUT
There's a lovely wine and tapas bar near us called Vino Tap; it has a great selection of wines, and you'll find all sorts of dogs in there. Then there's Halex, which is great for coffee or cocktails.

AWAY FROM IT ALL
Heckfield Place in Hampshire. We drive there, but you can also get the train. It's a beautiful hotel and dogs are very welcome.

JAMES KNAPPETT, SANDIA CHANG, AND PAXO

When it came to naming their white, black, and tan
Jack Russell and Yorkie mix, husband-and-wife team James
Knappett and Sandia Chang were stuck between Paxo and
Branston. "Of course, in our family, it had to be food-related,"
says Sandia, who, like James, has spent years working in top
restaurants around the world. The pair met at Per Se in
New York and from there moved to Noma in Copenhagen,
before relocating to London and co-founding Bubbledogs
and Kitchen Table in 2012. Suffolk-born James is the
executive head chef, while Sandia, who hails from California,
is the master sommelier. Their dog is part of the team, too.
And his name? In the end, they settled on one of James's
favourite ingredients: Paxo, like the pre-packaged sage-and-
onion stuffing mix.

Like many in the food and drink industry, James and Sandia dreamed of opening their own place, and when they arrived in London the opportunity presented itself. They were offered a space on fashionable Charlotte Street in Fitzrovia, a gourmet destination north of Soho. "We were given a location before we'd even agreed on what we were going to open," says Sandia. "I wanted a champagne bar and James wanted a fine-dining restaurant." After some back and forth, they compromised and opened two separate spaces in one spot: Bubbledogs, serving champagne and hot-dogs, and behind it, the tasting-menu concept Kitchen Table.

Running a restaurant is all-consuming, and for James and Sandia, having a dog has helped them find a balance. "It's been a lifesaver for us," says Sandia, looking back. "Our whole life revolved around the restaurant, so getting a dog gave us an excuse to talk about something else or forced us to take ten minutes out of our day to go for a walk." When they first got Paxo, he would come to work with them; he had his own cosy set-up in the office. On coffee and lunch breaks, James, Sandia, or their staff would take him around the block.

PLAYGROUND

James: Hampstead Heath. It's close to where we live in north London, and we scattered Noodle's ashes there, so it's important to us.

Sandia: The dogs who walk there, and their owners, are really friendly. You'll never run into a dog off the lead that isn't.

LOCAL HANGOUT

James: One of the bonuses of dog-walking on Hampstead Heath is that just off it are two of my favourite pubs, both of which let dogs in. There's the Bull and Last, which is really good for food, and just down the road there's the Southampton Arms, an ale and cider house.

DOG HACK

James: Treats. They're the only thing that makes life easier when it comes to Paxo. We tried to get him the best dog food out there and he turned his nose up at it. Now we give him a middle-of-the-range brand from Tesco that he just mops up. The treats are all from Pedigree Chum— I think it's like Coca-Cola for kids.

Before Paxo, there was Noodle, a toy poodle and dachshund mix, who sadly died in a road accident. "When we lost him, there was none of that, 'Oh, shall we get another dog?'" says James. "It was just, 'We have to fill this gap.'" They were keen to get another small dog suited to living in London, one they could carry on escalators, take on the tube, and, of course, bring to pubs and restaurants. Sandia started looking online, and soon James was cycling along the canal to meet their future pup. "I was speaking with the owner and Paxo just sat there chewing my shoelace the entire time," adds James, laughing. "We bonded."

Since then, a lot has changed. James and Sandia have moved to a Victorian townhouse with a garden in north London. They have two children, Shea and Ru. "We're lucky that Paxo is great with them, especially now our daughter is a raging toddler," says Sandia. "She'll grab his hair and his tail, and he just gets on with it." Other dogs, he'll take or leave. "He's a bit like me, he's become very picky about who he likes to mix with," says James. "He used to play with everyone when he was younger and just go and go and go. I think he's found his stride now and some dogs he'll play with, some he won't. He's got his own character."

James and Sandia's business has changed too. In 2020 they took the decision to transform Bubbledogs into an online shop selling champagne; for now, their main physical focus is the Michelin-starred Kitchen Table, which has expanded into the former Bubbledogs space. And the future? Time will tell. "When we first got a dog, I thought: It's not getting on the bed or any furniture," says James, laughing at how long that rule lasted. "Paxo has free run of the house; he comes everywhere with us." And of course, in a house filled with only the best ingredients, he eats well. "I'd give him anything; he's one of the family."

London has always been a city of dogs. In Clerkenwell, elegant whippets shiver on their way to an art exhibition. Mongrel geezers steal sausages and rule the East End with an iron paw. And then there are the dogs of the rich and famous, who swan around Hampstead Heath drinking doggycinos and planning ski holidays in Switzerland. All across the city, they've wagged and fetched and inspired noteworthy locals. Today, we're putting pups front and centre.

FOUR-LEGGED MUSES

WORDS BY
JAMES SHACKELL

ROWAN ATKINSON AND SPINEE

We probably wouldn't trust Mr. Bean with a pet (he famously entered his long-suffering teddy bear in a dog show once—it did not win). But Rowan Atkinson and his Labrador, Spinee, are a regular sight around Chelsea's leafy, zillion-dollar streets, where Range Rovers outnumber people and sourdough is £17 per loaf. By all accounts, Spinee has a pretty sweet life, getting rides in Atkinson's vintage car collection, hanging out at his country estate, and watching endless *Blackadder* re-runs on DVD (she agrees that Tim McInnerny is criminally underrated, clever girl).

HELENA BONHAM CARTER AND PABLO

Helena Bonham Carter has played some pretty oddball characters, so we kind of expected her to own an Irish wolfhound with a name like Hepzibah Nightshade, who only fetches during the full moon and haunts the moors of Devon, snacking on unwary tourists. Instead, she's got a very cute black-and-white Tibetan terrier named Pablo, who doesn't seem to possess any dark, occult powers, and has never eaten anyone (as far as we know). Bit of a letdown, really.

LORD BYRON AND BOATSWAIN

Lord Byron was kind of the original 18th-century punk rocker, only instead of greasy guitar riffs, he favoured poetry (which doesn't sound very punk rock, but he was doing tonnes of opium at the time, so…). He was also big on dogs. Especially big, hairy Newfoundland dogs. His favourite was Boatswain, a noble black-and-white creature, strong of jaw and firm of flank, who died of rabies (yikes) and got a special Byron poem inscribed on his marble tomb: *To mark a friend's remains these stones arise; / I never knew but one—and here he lies.* We're not crying. You're crying.

WINSTON CHURCHILL AND RUFUS

If there's a single dog responsible for the defeat of Nazism, it's Rufus, Winston Churchill's adorable poodle, who (legend says) was actually the one who came up with the whole fight-them-on-the-beaches line. Rufus followed Churchill throughout WWII, offering moral support, cuddles, and shrewd military tactics. Churchill took him to lunches and official meetings, and whenever Rufus wasn't invited, Churchill would always give him a good reason, e.g., "Apologies, Rufus. The Chancellor of the Exchequer is allergic, I hope you understand." After Rufus's death in 1947, Churchill got another poodle: Rufus II. He claimed the 'two' was silent.

LUCIAN FREUD AND PLUTO

What is it about 'modern art' pioneers? Just like Picasso, British artist Lucian Freud loved painting dogs and naked ladies, often on the same canvas (see: *Girl with a White Dog*, possibly one of the most unnecessary boobs ever rendered in oils). To be fair to Freud, it wasn't just the ladies: his canine obsession influenced pretty much all his work. "My liking to [paint] them naked is for that reason," he said. "I like my people to look as natural as animals." So… naked human animals, yep? Freud's doggy companion was the whippet Pluto, whom he sketched and painted all the way till her death in 2003. Naked, presumably.

PAUL McCARTNEY AND MARTHA

Paul McCartney's English sheepdog, Martha, is often called the fifth Beatle, which must really sting for Pete Best (the dude who left before they became famous). Martha's paw prints are all over the Beatles' early stuff. She was there at Strawberry Fields and got seasick in the Yellow Submarine. In 1968, McCartney recorded the piano track 'Martha My Dear' for the White Album, and everyone assumed he was singing about his ex. But nope, it was shaggy-haired Martha, the most famous sheepdog never used to advertise weatherproof paint. "Whereas it would appear… to be a song to a girl called Martha, it's actually a dog," Paul said, "and our relationship was platonic, believe me."

VIRGINIA WOOLF AND PINKA

Who's afraid of Virginia Woolf? Definitely not Pinka, her purebred cocker spaniel. Woolf actually had a bunch of dogs during her London life. There was a shaggy terrier named Shag (classic), a sheepdog named Gurth, and a boxer, Hans, whom Woolf taught to put out matches after lighting a cigarette, a trick she eventually taught all her pups. (When you're a genius novelist, getting your dogs to blow out matches isn't considered weird, just delightfully eccentric.) Pinka was the favourite, though, and even appeared on the cover of *Flush*, Woolf's fake biography of Elizabeth Barrett Browning's cocker spaniel. Like all good London dogs, Pinka goes down in history as a mutt— but also a muse. She inspired Woolf to the bitter end.

RESCUE ORGANISATIONS

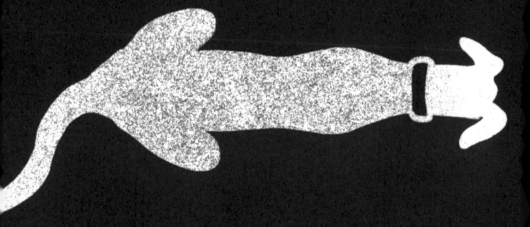

ALL DOGS MATTER

Rescuing dogs across Greater London as well as those overseas, this long-standing organisation is there for pups who lack a loving home.

ALLDOGSMATTER.CO.UK
@ALLDOGSMATTER

BARKING MAD DOG RESCUE

Barking Mad was born from a "that's enough" moment. The charity feeds, boards, and rehomes Romanian dogs who would otherwise spend their life in a shelter.

BARKINGMADDOGRESCUE.CO.UK
@BMDRDOGS

BATTERSEA DOGS AND CATS HOME

This dog (and cat) rescue has been rehoming our canine friends since 1860. That adds up to over three million animals now living their best life.

BATTERSEA.ORG.UK
@BATTERSEA

BLUECROSS

Bluecross has been looking after dogs since 1897. The team is ready to restore health and happiness to every pup they take in, whether injured, ill, or just unwanted.

BLUECROSS.ORG.UK
@THE_BLUE_CROSS

COOKIE'S RESCUE

This global organisation helps impoverished dogs in Lebanon find arms-stretched-wide owners in London.

COOKIESRESCUE.COM
@COOKIESRESCUE

DOGS TRUST

As the largest dog welfare charity in the UK, Dogs Trust not only rescues pups, but has also been successfully lobbying for canine rights for well over 125 years.

DOGSTRUST.ORG.UK
@DOGSTRUST

HUMANE SOCIETY

Funded entirely by individuals, the Humane Society provides a loving environment until our furry friends find adoring humans to take them home.

HSLM.CA
@HUMANESOCIETYLM

MAYHEW

Working to improve the lives of pups at home and abroad, Mayhew has been providing a broad range of veterinary and animal welfare services since 1886.

THEMAYHEW.ORG
@THEMAYHEW

OLDIES CLUB

This aptly named organisation rescues and rehomes dogs that are at least seven years old, proving these calmer canines still have plenty of love to give.

OLDIES.ORG.UK
@OLDIES_CLUB

PAWS RESCUE

Paws Rescue works to rehabilitate the growing number of abandoned animals in Qatar and find them a forever home in the UK.

PAWSRESCUEUK.ORG
@PAWSRESCUEUK

UNDERDOG INTERNATIONAL

Focused on the compassion a pup can bring into a home, Underdog links kids with canines to help with animal-assisted therapy, outreach programmes, and adoption.

THEUNDERDOG.ORG
@UNDERDOGINTERNATIONAL

WILD AT HEART

WAH is committed to helping as many of the 600 million strays in this world as possible, through sterilisation efforts, educational projects, and finding homes for dogs in need.

WILDATHEARTFOUNDATION.ORG
@WILD_AT_HEART_FOUNDATION

WOOD GREEN

Wood Green is here for the humans as well as the hounds. The charity offers expert pet advice and community workshops for people, and safe shelter for dogs without a home.

WOODGREEN.ORG.UK
@WOODGREEN.THEANIMALSCHARITY

INDEX

DOG-FRIENDLY LONDON

First edition

Co-Creators—
WINNIE AU
MARTA ROCA

Creative Direction and Design—
MARTA ROCA

Photography—
LESLEY LAU
DUNJA OPALKO
ARIANA RUTH

Editor-at-Large—
KAREN DAY

Writers—
CHLOË ASHBY
KAREN DAY
OLIVIA FINLAYSON
HANNAH SUMMERS

Illustrations—
PAULINE CREMER

Copy Editor—
MEREDITH FORRESTER

Dog-friendly City Guides
©2021 Winnie Au and Marta Roca

Photography
©Lesley Lau
©Dunja Opalko
©Ariana Ruth

First published in 2021
by Hoxton Mini Press, London
in collaboration with Four&Sons

hoxtonminipress.com
fourandsons.com

A CIP catalogue record for this book
is available from the British Library.

Hoxton Mini Press is an environmentally
conscious publisher, committed
to offsetting our carbon footprint.
The offset for this book was purchased
from Stand For Trees.

This book was printed on paper
certified by the FSC®

ISBN: 978-1-910566-91-6

Printed and bound by OZGraf, Poland

MIX
Paper from
responsible sources
FSC
www.fsc.org
FSC® C163799

SPECIAL THANKS—

Anna and Joseph Au
Cindy Au and Callan Lamb
Florent Bariod
Ashley Ball
Libby Borton
Anthony Burrill
Paz Castro
Pauline Cremer
Andie Cusick
Niko Dafkos
Karen Day
Paul Firmin
Meredith Forrester
Aurelie Four
Alessandra Genualdo
Genesta Gunn
Travis Garone
Ash James
Una Maguire
Jenny Matthews
Daniel McCabe
Sara Meissner
Faye Mitchell
Sally Muir
Nadja Occam Penfold
Alice and Stuart Quan
Luis Reina Romao
Bonnie Saporetti
Fiona Smith
Hannah Summers
Cristina Torras
Martin Usborne
Ann Waldvogel

DOG FRIENDS—

Thanks to all the Londoners
featured in this guide and
to all the dogs for being such
a source of joy and friendship.

FOUR&SONS   HOXTON MINI PRESS